GOD'S WILDERNESS

GOD'S WILDERNESS

Discoveries in Sinai

BENO ROTHENBERG

in collaboration with *Yohanan Aharoni*
and Avia Hashimshoni
90 photogravure plates   16 maps and plans

THOMAS NELSON & SONS

New York   *Toronto*

Translated from the Hebrew by Joseph Witriol.

THIS EDITION © THAMES AND HUDSON 1961
FIRST AMERICAN EDITION THOMAS NELSON & SONS 1962
LIBRARY OF CONGRESS CATALOGUE CARD NUMBER 62 - 7976
TEXT PRINTED BY JOH. ENSCHEDÉ EN ZONEN HAARLEM HOLLAND
ILLUSTRATIONS PRINTED BY BRAUN ET CIE MULHOUSE FRANCE
BOUND BY VAN RIJMENAM N.V. THE HAGUE HOLLAND.

Contents

FOREWORD   The Sinai peninsula was open to exploration and study by Israeli scholars for only a few months, in the winter of 1956–57; but in this brief period probably more intensive research was carried out on the territory than at any previous time in its history. Research expeditions were undertaken as occasion offered by persons acting in a private capacity and also by organized teams from Israeli Institutes of Higher Learning. Four expeditions were conducted in southern Sinai; two under the direction of Professor B. Mazar, President of the Hebrew University, and one led by Mr S. Yeivin, Director of the Department of Antiquities; in a fourth expedition conducted by scholars from a number of different departments the undersigned was in charge of archaeological research. Two expeditions explored northern Sinai: one organized by the Department of Antiquities under Mr M. Dothan, and the other organized by the Hebrew University under my direction. Of the private expeditions, the most important were those undertaken by Shmarya Gutman of Naan, and Beno Rothenberg, the archaeologist and photographer.

The results of some of the researches conducted on these expeditions are published for the first time in this book. Each contributor is responsible for the opinions he expresses. The reader will notice that occasionally contributors hold different views on given finds, though they agree, of course, on the archaeological data themselves. The reader is free to make his own choice.

It will necessarily be some considerable time before the mass of material gathered on these expeditions can be properly evaluated and recorded in various specialist publications. Accordingly, I have more or less confined myself, in my paper on 'Kadesh-barnea and Mount Sinai' to a consideration of the central problem that has never ceased to engage the attention of layman and scholar alike: the identification of the Mountain of God and of the route taken by the Children of Israel in their wandering through the wilderness.

We are far from claiming to have solved all the problems and difficulties of Sinai research. We are conscious of the debt we owe to our predecessors in the field. Without the great volume of important research published in the last hundred, and particularly the last fifty years, our own conclusions would have been incomplete, and, indeed, sometimes unintelligible. We may, however, hope that in this book we have thrown a fresh light on our subject and that our identifications of the Peninsula's oases, mountains and roads will lead to a deeper understanding of the special role played by the Wilderness of Sinai in the history of the Jewish People.

In any case, the reports of our findings published here cannot but be subsidiary to the book's photographs. It is these which reveal to us the Sinai desert with all its buried treasure, its tantalizing secrets and its wild and wonderful splendour.

YOHANAN AHARONI

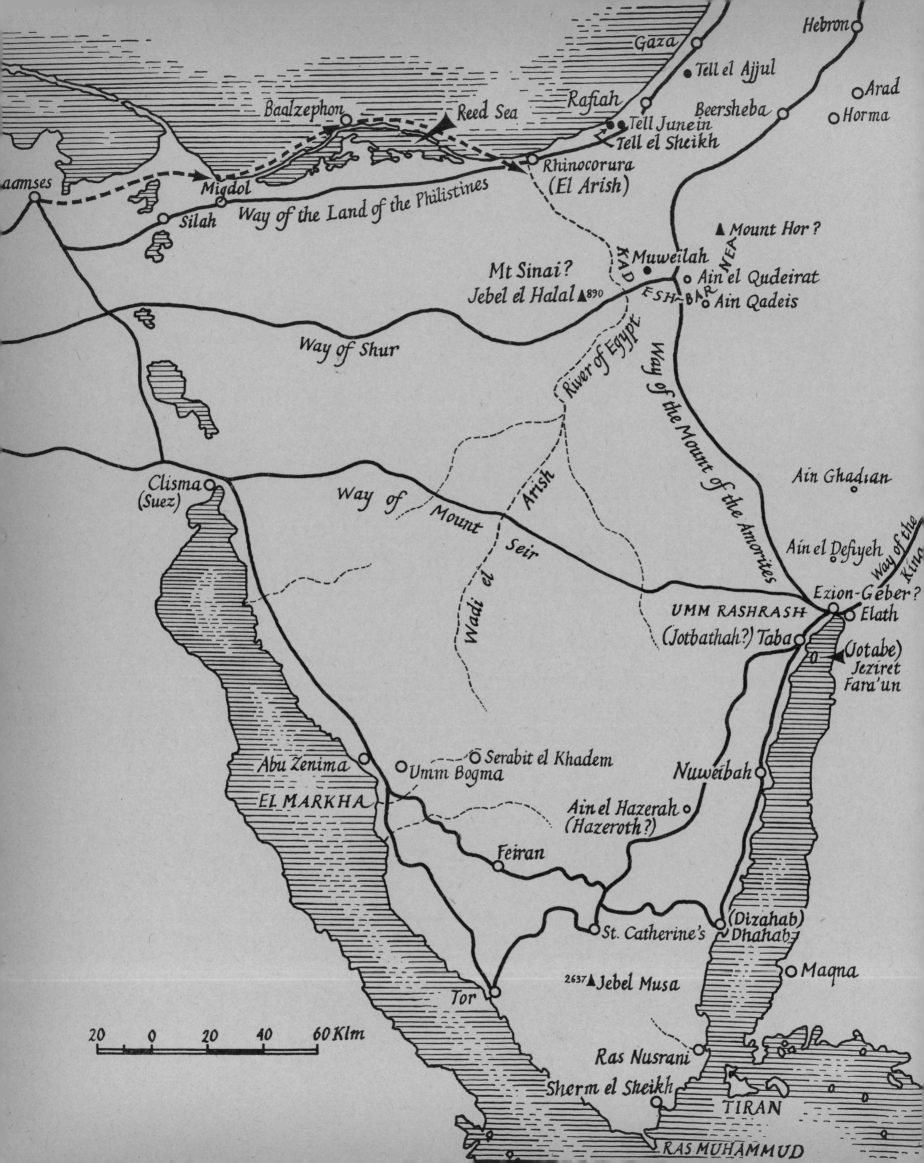

INTRODUCTION

To the memory of my father, Chaim Jacob ben Mordechai, who guided my first steps in the paths of the heavenly Sinai

Many travellers have passed through Sinai, from the early Middle Ages onwards. Mostly they travelled by camel or on the humble ass. Some even walked the whole way, along the traditional route from Suez via Abu Zenima to Tor, and thence via Wadi Hebran to the enchanting monastery of St Catherine's. Many succeeded in climbing the mountains of Sinai, and at considerable hazard made the perilous ascent of Jebel Musa or Ras Safsafa in order to trace the footsteps of Moses when he ascended the Mountain of God.

The books they wrote breathe the spirit of romanticism. There is the still, cold desert night, the starry sky, the Beduin guide enveloped in his loose, picturesque *abaye*, squatting by the small camp fire which he feeds with dry, aromatic twigs, while from time to time he puffs at the long stem of a pipe richly decorated with oriental carving. Frequently we read of encounters, not always peaceful, with merchant caravans, with smugglers, desperadoes whose eyes flash fire as they draw their long scimitars. There is the ceremonial coffee, of course, drunk by the son of the local Sheikh and his English 'brother'; on another occasion the young host beats off with tremendous bravery a gang of Beduin who threaten to exterminate his honoured guests. Needless to say, the traditional hospitality of even the poorest Beduin, who invariably slaughter their last sheep in honour of the passing guest, is given its due place in the story.

My book is not of this kind. It tells the story of a modern traveller who covered long distances at the wheel of a car, and sometimes on board ship or in a planc. From 29th October 1956, when the Sinai campaign started, to 20th January 1957 I utilized every opportunity, every free day, every kind or vehicle—car, Jeep or Piper Cub—to penetrate again and again into the stillness of this great Sinai desert, to wander over these empty but beautiful lands with their deep, barely negotiable wadis.

In their tens of thousands Israel's youth also took the opportunity to sweep into the Peninsula. The spectacle of these khaki-clad youngsters, boys and girls, exploring Sinai, made an unforgettable impression on us. As far south as, roughly, the ancient route from Suez to Eilat I was able to travel fairly easily, accompanied by a few friends, in my faithful Land-Rover. Because of this comparative ease of travel, this central region of the Peninsula was the main scene of our photographic and archaeological activities. We concentrated particularly on the area of Kadesh-barnea (Ain el Qudeirat—Ain Qadeis—El Qusaima—El Muweilah) and along the route Eilat—

Fig. 1. General map of the Sinai Peninsula

Qal'at el Nakhl—Mitla Pass southwards down to Ras el Sudr and the region south and west of Eilat.

Geologists, botanists, zoologists and others, as well as archaeologists and epigraphists, were able to make use of the opportunity—all too short, alas!—for scientific study. Many Israeli scientists, particularly the younger ones, were able to carry out their researches in the remotest parts of the Peninsula: in St Catherine's Monastery and in the mangrove growth at the southernmost tip of the Gulf of Eilat (Aqaba); in the 'River of Egypt' (Wadi el Arish) and in the steep rocks of Ain Qadeis. In the limited time that was available for unhampered research much good work was done, and there is no doubt that when the extensive material that has been gathered is sifted and evaluated an important contribution will have been made to Sinaitic studies in many fields.

A research team from the Hebrew University in Jerusalem, among them Professors Mazar, Polotzky, Meir, Pravor, Ben Chorin and others, spent some time in the library of St Catherine's, devoting special attention to the part played by Sinai's monasteries in the early history of Palestine.

I was not a member of the University expedition, but by courtesy of Professor Mazar I was able to join it for a trip to the manganese mines of Umm Bogma and to the ancient Egyptian port of El Markha. Dr Yohanan Aharoni, Hebrew University, also went to southern Sinai to carry out archaeological research. He was able to re-examine some sites already known to archaeologists, and also to examine some which have not yet been the subject of archaeological study. He succeeded in exploring the lonely island of Tiran, identified by many scholars with Jotabe. He was able to show that this island had never been permanently inhabited and that its identification with Jotabe did not accord with the archaeological evidence. Dr Aharoni also carried out work on the ancient remains of El Markha, where he found remains additional to those discovered by Professor Albright in 1948. In the enchanting oasis of Dhahab, too, on the shore of the Gulf of Eilat (Aqaba), he found ancient remains of great historical interest.

Towards the end of the period of unrestricted movement in the Peninsula I joined a study group of Hebrew University undergraduates led by Dr Aharoni. This group concentrated on the ancient tells on the northern coast of Sinai, from Gaza to El Arish. As a member of this group I found myself again, for perhaps the sixth or seventh time, in the Kadesh-barnea region. Together with Dr Aharoni and his pupils I explored once more the ancient sites in Wadi el Ain (Qudeirat). We covered the whole length of the wall (the northern part) which surrounds the wadi on the slopes of Jebel el Ain and we inspected the various ancient Israelite forts and watch-towers as well as the Canaanite settlements (Middle Bronze Age I 2,100–1,900 B.C.) which my group had found on its previous expeditions. Although in the course of this expedition with Dr Aharoni and his group I was able to gain further valuable information, I felt I ought to pay this region yet another visit. And so, while the army's withdrawal was still on, perhaps a day or so after it had ended, we set out— my two companions, Hebrew University undergraduates, and I—from Beerotaim (Birein) and walked the whole length of Jebel el Ain up to a point overlooking the glorious springs. On this expedition we were able to discover, survey and photograph a further number of ancient sites, mostly dating from the beginning of the time of the Patriarchs (MB I).

In many cases the accounts of my predecessors helped me to find places of extraordinary interest and beauty. I could not help being struck by the great changes which had taken place, in the last century or two, not merely in individual sites, but in whole landscapes. It is true, of course, that it was not only the scenery that had changed; the observer's viewpoint had changed, too. An Israeli in 1957 inevitably saw Sinai with different eyes from those with which Christian observers in the nineteenth or eighteenth centuries saw it. Among the travellers in the great wilderness there were of course many gifted with keen powers of scientific observation who reported accurately on their discoveries. It will suffice to mention the names of Palmer, Robinson, Lepsius, Stanley, Lawrence, Woolley and Petrie. Nevertheless, the state of scientific knowledge at the time prevented them—in the majority of cases—from making accurate identifications, and the powers of judgement of previous travellers in the region were obscured by theories of scriptural inspiration. Moreover, fundamental changes had taken place in Sinai within the last few generations. There were times when it seemed to me that the very air had changed. On the one hand I saw neglect, on the other industrialization or abortive attempts to change the character of the inhabitants: a beautiful spring (Ain el Qudeirat) covered up with an ugly structure of reinforced concrete, a purling stream forced into a strait-jacket of iron pipes, nomadic Beduin shepherds turned into peasants tied to the soil.

The Bible was my faithful companion on all my Sinai travels, but on more than one occasion my camera came into conflict with it. I found myself compelled to adjust my preconceived notions of the country and its people to the evidence of my view-finder. Biblical associations yielded to the visual reality. For example, after much searching for the Biblical fountain of Marah we eventually reached the spring of Ain Hawara. Previous travellers had described this as a 'beautiful spring of water', but the camera recorded a scene of desolation, a solitary dismal palm-tree in a sea of swirling sand dunes. The sense of disillusion was profound. Even so, in my innermost being I had 'lived' something that was quite different from the photographic record: 'the waters of Marah' of the Exodus from Egypt.

I have sub-titled this book *Discoveries in Sinai*, not because of the archaeological discoveries made by the various Israeli expeditions, including my own, but because innumerable Israelis of the present generation who were privileged to follow 'in the footsteps' of their Israelite ancestors discovered in Sinai the rock whence they were hewn. My camera supplied the most important material for my notebook. Hence this volume illustrates and describes many important sites in all parts of Sinai, but it does not attempt to show the whole of the Sinai peninsula. In choosing the photographs for reproduction in this book we selected, from more than three thousand which I took in Sinai, pictures of sites, scenes and objects which had not been photographed before or had been photographed unsatisfactorily. Although most of the important sites in Sinai have been included, to enable the photographs to lay some claim to comprehensiveness, in all cases the quality of the picture was the decisive consideration. Many sites, previously unknown, were revealed by us for the first time and are therefore included in the photographs here reproduced.

In presenting this book to the reader my intention was not so much to place before him an illustrated text-book on the history and geography of Sinai, as to convey to him as far as I could something of the *genius loci*, of the unique atmosphere that pervades these desolate expanses and broods mysteriously over these mighty granite mountains.

I have to thank many people for making this book possible. Chiefly Dr Y. Aharoni who undertook the redaction of the complete text without, however, seeking to make the opinions of his fellow contributors conform to his own. I am indebted to M. Jean Perrot, the French archaeologist, for re-examining the flint implements we collected; to Avia Hashimshoni for his important paper, and to Professor A. Shalit, Dr B. Segal and Mr B. Sapir for deciphering the newly discovered inscriptions. Mr Menasseh Kehilla prepared most of the figures and maps in the book; the remainder were compiled by Miss Esther Kaufman and Mr Kollodni. I have to thank my colleagues Isaac Herbst and A. Vered for their help, also Mr Mark Shraga, who was in charge of the processing of the photographs.

My thanks are also extended to those many good companions who accompanied me on my Sinai expeditions. Here I can only mention: Yehuda Freedman, Danny Litt, Leah Ofer, Yerucham Luria and Shmuel Katz. I am also indebted to the following members of the *Kibbutz Artzi* organization: Yoash Yedidiah (who also read the notes on the plates), Bezalel Canaan, Eliezer Friedmann, Ben Ammi Gaon, Ziva Meltzer. I am grateful to many members of the Israeli Army, particularly Col. Abraham Yoffe and Col. Uzi Narkiss who gave me wise counsel and practical help on my expeditions. Mgr Akiva Saar gave me valuable assistance in St Catherine's Monastery.

TEL AVIV   BENO ROTHENBERG

SINAI NOTEBOOK

BENO ROTHENBERG

PART ONE   EN ROUTE

Early on the morning of 9th November 1956 five of us set out southwards from Beersheba in a Land-Rover on a hastily-improvised expedition into what was, for us, unknown territory. With only one vehicle we could not risk going too far south, so we decided to make first for Ain el Qudeirat, and then to cross the vast plateau of central Sinai, the 'Wilderness of the Wanderings' reaching the Gulf of Suez at the modern oil city of Ras el Sudr.

The road to the Sinai boundary by-passes the ruined, once-great cities of Halutza (Khalassa) and Rehovoth Banegeb (Ruheiba) now choked with sand which swirls continuously from the shore over these and other early settlements. We passed dismantled barracks and disused railway stations, relics of the Turkish and British occupations, as well as some trim, new Israeli settlements. At the foot of a steep mountain, El Mushrifa, on the summit of which is a Nabataean-Byzantine fortress, the road turns sharply to wind its way upwards along a narrow wadi, emerging on a broad golden-coloured plain traversed by the broad beds of dried-up watercourses and studded with hillocks set widely apart. We stopped for a while near 'Shallah', a new settlement about eight miles from Nitzana, at the foot of a hillside strewn with gleaming flint. We had previously found prehistoric flint implements here (Israeli grid co-ordinates: 035–108) and now wished to collect more specimens. My companions searched enthusiastically and soon gathered a great pile of Upper Palaeolithic flint implements. They were beautiful tools covered with a light-brown desert patina, and of marvellously accurate craftsmanship. Their existence did not come as a surprise, as we knew from previous explorations that the mountains of the Negeb were in general a treasure-house of interesting prehistoric implements. In the course of our own investigations it became clear to us that this was true of Sinai, too. There is of course no real boundary—historical, archaeological or geographical—between the Negeb and Sinai until the 'River of Egypt' (Wadi el Arish) is reached.

Here, I will digress to describe another early site encountered on a later expedition, on 20th February 1957, on the way to Sinai. Our route lay through Wadi Arabah on the way to Eilat, and our plan was to investigate a number of sites of archaeological interest in the region, and from these to continue via Ras el Nagb along the 'Pilgrim's Way' (Darb el Haj) to eastern Sinai. We followed the ancient route Beersheba—Kefar Jeroham—Mamshit (Kurnub), etc., as I wanted to photograph the new dam at Kefar Jeroham (in Wadi Rekhme) after it had been filled by the recent rains. We left the road after passing the 'tell' of Rekhme and continued along a track that led straight to the ancient well of Bir Rekhme. As we drove south along Wadi Jurf, our heavily loaded Jeep bumping over the low, rolling hills, my attention was suddenly aroused by some interesting sherds I saw lying on the ground. I made a preliminary examination without being able to reach any firm conclusions. Some of the sherds were Middle Bronze I and others seemed later, one or two even suggesting pottery dating from the Judaean kingdom. We continued our search and in a short while were rewarded by finding the clear foundations of a circular building, about seven to eight yards in diameter, on the summit of one of the hills. To have attempted to date this structure by reference to the mass of mixed early and Byzantine sherds lying around would have been hopeless. However, we refused to despair. Where there were early sherds there was bound to be an early settlement not far away. I carefully scanned every hill within sight and, on a low ridge of Mt Rahama (Jebel Rekhme) on the other side of Wadi Jurf, spotted some structures which on subsequent examination proved to be tombs of early Patriarchal date, and a rampart on a high ridge above. In the early light of morning it was clearly visible in the distance.

We decided to inspect the newly discovered site. The wadi being in spate, we had to return to the road and drive back along it towards Beersheba for about half a mile and then, skirting the whole plain, approach the dam from the north.

We crossed the dam and began searching the steep slopes of Jebel Rekhme. The structures were on top of a narrow rock rising to a height of some few yards in the centre of the slope, about 110 yards above the level of the wadi. We found sherds as soon as we reached the site; all were Middle Bronze I. The structures were fairly clear, too; tombs, partly broken up by the action of man or beast, partly eroded by time.

We went on up to the top of the hill—a steep climb. On this upper slope, too, we collected a number of sherds, again all MB I. At the top a surprise awaited us! We were standing about 500 feet above the level of the wadi. The flat hill-top was surrounded by a strong wall of unhewn stone. A space between the wall and the rock forming the summit of the hill had been filled in to make a great platform. In the middle of this platform a huge bare rock rose dramatically to a height of seven feet. The first thing that struck us was the six large cup-marks hollowed out of the rock. It was with a thrill of excitement that we realised we had discovered the first Canaanite sanctuary in the Negeb   the great stone in the middle left us in no doubt that we were face to face with a Canaanite 'High Place'.

This site differed completely from all others of the same period previously discovered in the Negeb. Hitherto no site dating from the beginning of the Patriarchal period (MB I) had been discovered with a high, solid wall around it; no strongly fortified settlement on a barely accessible hill-top.

The platform was about 90 feet in diameter and the wall rose in places to a height of 6½ feet (external measurements). The wall was not of uniform thickness, nor was it perfectly circular in shape, following as it did the natural features of the hill-top. A clear path led straight from the 'daiga' (the wadi in which the dam was situated) to the sanctuary. There was no masonry within the wall or near it except the natural rock, with the large cup-marks, in the middle.

From here we could see that the neighbouring slopes were studded with ruins. The hill somewhat resembling a crooked table that rose to the north of us, in particular, seemed a veritable fortress. From our vantage point we could clearly follow the line of the wall from the hill-top to the side facing the wadi.

*Fig. 2-3. The Canaanite sanctuary and settlement on Jebel Rekhme:
(1) the platform, (2) the walled settlement, (3) isolated tombs,
(4) hill with large tombs, (5) buildings and tombs*

We realized that we should be unable to go any further for the day, and decided to spend the time till dusk in examining our discovery. Even at this stage we knew that what we had discovered here was a key to the Canaanite settlements of the Negeb hills.

Fig. 2-3 The steep slope west of the 'sanctuary' too was strewn with typical MB I buildings: circular or rectangular ruins, some joined to each other. In addition, there were large quantities of sherds of the types known to us from sites of this period. The slope descended about 100 feet and then rose as a narrow shelf forming, as it were, a saddle leading to the high hill on the north. This eminence, too, was full of ruins and sherds. In particular some well-built tombs about 3 feet high and about 13–16 feet in diameter caught our eye. Eventually we climbed the large hill to the north, collecting more sherds—all MB I—on the way.

The settlement on the top of this hill had been deliberately destroyed. Many settlements of this period in the Negeb convey the impression of having been simply abandoned by their inhabitants, but this, however, planned and fortified as it was, had been razed to the ground and part of the stonework used to construct tombs. In some places the wall itself had been demolished and its stones used for tombs, perhaps for the burial of the settlement's warriors among its ruins after it had been destroyed by the enemy. But who were the inhabitants of the site? And who the conqueror? Did the Amorite dwell here when Abraham sojourned in the Negeb? Was the settlement conquered in the campaign of the four kings headed by Chedorlaomer, king of Elam (Gen. xiv.i.)?

The site, which is about 375 feet long, is divided into two parts. It is surrounded by the clear remains of a casemate wall. The upper part was used for dwellings and probably, at a later date, for large tombs. It is interesting to note that the largest tomb has next to it a smooth rock with a number of large cup-marks and many more very small ones. The dwellings have their courtyards attached, indicating a well-organized settlement. The lower part of the settlement was presumably intended for communal use; it is merely a large courtyard divided in two by an internal wall. In the courtyard are ruins next to a cup-marked rock. The site is strewn with numerous sherds and flint implements. Sherds and ruins are all indubitably MB I.[1]

From here the whole plain of Rekhme lies as if stretched out on the palm of a hand, and the most distant features can be clearly seen. Perhaps this site was chosen for the erection of the sanctuary in the past because it was visible from great distances. Smoke and fire can be distinguished from as far off as Mamshit (Kurnub) to the east and the distant hills in the south.

I pictured to myself the busy life that must have gone on here at various periods in the long history of the Negeb, and I asked my companions: 'Is it conceivable that an area as thickly settled and populated as the area of Tell Rekhme should have been completely passed over in the Bible?' It was not till some little time later, when I was putting my Sinai experiences into writing, that a possible answer to my question occurred to me: the name Rekhme, which has no lexical significance, of course, in Arabic, is simply an echo of the name Jerahmeal, and the Tell Rekhme area (the modern Kefar Jeroham) is simply the 'Negeb of the Jerahmeelites'.[2]

In the Canaanite era, of course, there were no roads in the Negeb in the modern sense; merely tracks following more or less fixed traditional routes. Hence the route from Kadesh-barnea to Hormah, which was the path of the first Israelite invasion of Canaan, probably passed through the district of Bir Hafir, and continued on to the region of Rekhme before striking north-eastwards to reach a spot near Tell Melhata, the Biblical Hormah, in the plain of Beersheba.

I now resume the narrative of our 1956 expedition. We continued along the Beersheba-Nitzana road, heading south-west for the Sinai border. We passed Qetziot, a new settlement near the international boundary line, and in a few minutes came to a high hill, Nitzana (Auja el Hafir), the main road-junction between Israel and Sinai. Here four main roads meet from all points of the compass.

The gleaming white hill of Nitzana stands out from a broad complex of wadis. Nitzana (the ancient name of Auja el Hafir was ascertained with the help of Greek documents found in the ruins of the city by an archaeological expedition headed by Colt, in 1935–36) has undergone many vicissitudes in its long history. In the Byzantine era (5th and 6th centuries A.D.), it was an important city numbering some 10,000 souls; in the First World War it was an important military base for the Turks, from which they planned to capture the Suez Canal; subsequently it declined into a small settlement of the Azazmeh Beduin in the period of the British mandate of Palestine.

We climbed up the hill of the fortress. We could have continued driving quite safely along the Ismailia or Beerotaim (Birein)-El Qusaima road, had we wished, but decided to stay for a short time at Nitzana. Standing on the wall of the Byzantine fortress of Nitzana we were able to command a view over fairly wide distances. The hill on which the fortress was built stands at the intersection of two wadis; the broad, gleaming wadi of Ezuz (Azeizi), and Wadi Hafir which winds its way from the coastal sand-strip to a point near Jebel el Ain in the south. In ancient times these two wadis in the hills of the western Negeb were important lines of communication bordered by large settlements. Nelson Glueck's expedition made a thorough survey of this region, investigating numerous important remains of

[1] A detailed account of all these finds will be given in my forthcoming book on the history of the Negeb.

[2] While reading the proofs of the first Hebrew edition of this book (October, 1957) I came across *Our Work in Palestine*, published in 1873 by the Palestine Exploration Fund. This book contains a brief account of a journey made by Palmer and Drake in the desert of Et Tih and the Negeb. The authors endeavoured to identify the various regions of the Negeb as they were known in the time of David: the Negeb of Judah, the Negeb of the Cherethites, the Negeb of Caleb, the Negeb of the Kenites and the Negeb of the Jerahmeelites. Judge of my surprise to learn that the identification Tell Rekhme with the Negeb of the Jerahmeelites was not original at all. 'Any tolerably competent linguist will see that Jebel Rekhme is an echo of the name Negeb of the Jerahmeelites. Between Wadi Rekhme in the north and Wadi el Abeid . . . in the south lies the Negeb of the Jerahmeelites.' (cf. also Yohanan Aharoni: 'The Negeb of Judah,' in *Israel Exploration Journal*, 8, 1958, pp. 26-38.)

settlements, mostly dating from the beginning of the Patriarchal period, from the united monarchy and the Judaean kingdom and from the Nabataean and later periods.[1] As we stood, then, viewing the region from the heights of Nitzana, we had yet to learn that this area of roads and settlements extends in actual fact beyond the boundary line to the mountain range of Jebel Mushraq and Jebel el Abyad, and, within certain limits, even to Jebel el Halal. The whole of this area is geographically and geologically and, particularly, archaeologically homogeneous: everywhere are the same early settlements, the same fortifications dating from the Hebrew monarchy, the same water-holes and ancient terraces designed to retain the soil and drain off the rainwater. Moreover, even before the dawn of history man had dwelt here. On many of the hill-tops in the region Palaeolithic flint implements had been discovered. North of Nitzana, scattered around some stone circles on the east side of Wadi Ezuz, fine late-Neolithic (c. 5,000 B.C.) flint implements have been discovered. These implements comprise, chiefly, superbly fashioned arrow-heads, blades, scrapers, and other artifacts. The men who used these implements do not appear to have engaged in agriculture but to have been nomadic hunters. They would have stayed at this spot awhile because of its good supply of subterranean water; perhaps, also, because of the local green flint, which was easy to work in.

The discovery of these remains in the arid region of the Negeb wadis had come as a major surprise to all of us, as did the subsequent filling-in on the map, in the course of a few years' surveying, of numerous historic settlements whose existence had never previously been suspected. There are a number of early settlements in the Negeb dating from the time of Abraham (21st–19th centuries B.C.), but it is in the region bordering Kadesh-barnea that the chief area of settlement was in all probability located. It is difficult to wander over the hills and escarpments along Wadis Ezuz and Nitzana without encountering remains of settlements, all laid out on a similar pattern: courtyards with a low wall of unhewn stone and small circular structures inside the wall or close by outside. On many sites a large upright stone stands built into the wall of the courtyard or structure; in a few instances a smooth cup-marked rock nearby has been discovered. The inhabitants of these villages were probably shepherds who also tilled the wadi-beds around their settlements.

We found another site of particular interest, both because of its similarity to, and difference from, the large Canaanite settlement near Kefar Jeroham already mentioned. In contrast to the sanctuary and settlement on Jebel Rekhme, this site was not fortified and is situated on a broad, easily accessible spit of land between two wadis (Nitzana and Ezuz). In all likelihood this was the chief settlement of the region in the Middle Bronze I period.

From where we stood on the wall of the citadel of Nitzana we were unable, even in the strong sunlight, to pick out this settlement, which lies about $2\frac{1}{2}$ miles east of Beerotaim. The wadi-beds, strewn with gravel and stone, were dazzlingly bright, but to discern the actual remains of the settlement we had to approach to within a few score yards of the site, which had been completely destroyed—the walls that remained were only a foot or so in height. The town, which by the standards of the time was one of major importance, was well-planned, with roads and streets. The dwellings and courtyards were 'classical' in pattern: circular or rectangular buildings with courtyards attached. Here, however, instead of the single dwelling and courtyard which are to be found in their thousands in the Negeb, hundreds of such dwellings had been built adjoining each other to form a

[1] BASOR, 131 (1953), 137 (1955), 138 (1955), 142 (1956), 145 (1957).

large urban settlement. We may assume that the site served as a 'metropolis' for all the settlements of the period in this part of the Negeb up to the fringe of Canaanite settlement west of Kadesh-barnea.

A brief comparison of this town at Wadis Nitzana and Ezuz with the settlement on Jebel Rekhme is instructive. It was built and destroyed at the beginning of the Middle Bronze period. This is proved both by the dwellings on the site and by the sherds we collected in its streets. Like all the other settlements of this period, it flourished in an era of prolonged peace. Not a single fortified settlement of this period has been found in the Negeb. All the Negeb settlements are 'open towns', with the exception of the large settlement on Jebel Rekhme. The impression given is that here both the sanctuary and the settlement on the mountain were built on the marches of the Negeb hills in an almost inaccessible, easily defensible spot. It is true that nearby are scores of scattered 'dwelling-units' with no defensive wall around them, but the main settlement was obviously within the fortified casemate walls. No doubt in time of trouble every one in the neighbouring region gathered here for safety. It is interesting to note that it was precisely this main settlement which was violently razed to the ground, whereas many of the isolated dwellings appear to have been vacated and left to decay with process of time.

Our site lay not far off the Nitzana-Beerotaim-El Qusaima road. We have grounds for assuming that the ancient road of the Middle Bronze period, of the Exodus and of the United Monarchy ran nearby. This assumption finds dramatic corroborative evidence in another site, recently discovered. Both on account of its intrinsic importance and because of the light it sheds on the mysterious wall in Wadi el Qudeirat I append here a description of it.[1]

The site is located approximately midway between Bir Birein and Bir Hafir, near the ancient road that ran from Kadesh-barnea to the Negeb, at the junction of Wadi Hafir and Wadi Horeishah. It lies on a low flat hill in the middle of an extensive plain and can be seen at a distance from all points of the compass. The site, which is unusually large, about 25 acres in area, is orientated NW to SE. The table-top of the hill is about 550 yards long and 220 yards wide. The greatest part of this hill-top is enclosed by a very stout well-built wall of unhewn stones, about 2 feet 8 inches to 3 feet 3 inches thick and about 3 feet 3 inches to 3 feet 8 inches high.

The building of this wall must have constituted a major enterprise. Its purpose is not easy to fathom. It has five 'entrances'. It is not high enough to serve for defence—we are convinced that in many places the wall still stands at its original height. The only logical explanation for the large number of entrances is that they were designed to facilitate ingress. At all events, a massive wall of this nature could not possibly have served to pen sheep or camels.

We considered the possibility that the wall might have served to conserve and direct rainwater. There is indeed a channel, constructed in comparatively recent times, from the hill-top down the eastern slope, leading to a water cistern. On the other hand, the hill-top slopes in such a way that it is quite obvious that the water would have gathered mainly *outside* the wall, where the silt left behind rises about 8–12 inches higher than the level of the ground inside the wall.

Since this great wall, encompassing as it does an area of some twenty-five acres, served neither for defence, nor for the collection and canalization of water, nor as a sheepfold—it can be assumed that it was constructed in view of the exceptional importance of the site itself. This must have been a sacred place, *sui generis*.

[1] See BASOR 145 (1957) p. 20 and Dr Aharoni's paper, pp. 138 ff.

No site resembling it has been found as yet in the Negeb, and very few elsewhere. (One such site is Bab edh-Dhra, discovered by Professor Albright on a hill slope east of the Dead Sea.)

There are practically no other remains of buildings within the walled enclosure except two huge stone circles. Evidently the whole area must have been one vast cemetery. A superficial dig turned up a few pottery vessels that were almost intact beneath a few inches of soil. They were of various periods: Iron Age II, Roman Byzantine, and some MB I sherds.[1]

In this arid catalogue of remains, masonry, conjectural routes, the interest of this huge, enigmatic ancient cemetery stands out. On this hill-top that stands at the intersection of two broad wadis covered with gleaming loess and low shrubs, with flints and pebbles, hundreds—perhaps thousands—of early Israelites have been 'gathered to their fathers': semi-nomads who died in the Negeb in the beginning of the Patriarchal period and were brought to the Holy Mountain from afar off; wanderers of the Exodus who camped near the springs of Kadesh-barnea and to whom a sight of the Promised Land was never to be vouchsafed.

We descended the Nitzana hill and drove on to Beerotaim. Around this new settlement, which lies on the hill-side near the well, are numerous early remains. Even in the courtyard it is possible to collect a multitude of Palaeolithic flint implements, while on the western side of the settlement's hill, above the eastern arm of Wadi Ezuz, which splits up here into numerous branches, there are remains of extensive settlements from the time of Abraham's wandering in the Negeb (Middle Bronze Age I). Most of the ridges in this region are studded with these remains. On a hill-top near the new settlement's farmland, we also found a small citadel dating from the Hebrew monarchy and, on a low hill-top south-west of the farm, a second fortress of the same period: a small square building with strong walls of unhewn stone. On the slopes of this second hill we found a few crude sherds. Remains of later periods also abound in this region. The terraces in the wadis and the large surrounding fences are particularly noticeable; the work of agricultural settlers—Judaean, Nabataean, Roman and Byzantine. Leaving Beerotaim, we drove on, across a lush plain and through a narrow pass between the small mountains of Jebel es Sabha (1,371 feet) and the hills south of the road (1,299 feet) to emerge on the other side of the frontier.

Only the boundary-post on a nearby hill and the barbed wire on either side of the road told us that we had passed into the territory of Sinai. In the landscape itself nothing had changed: the colouring, the loess soil, the limestone hills and the sand were exactly the same. Further on, west of the Kadesh-barnea region, there is, indeed, a noticeable difference. There, the boundary is a natural one, a boundary between the wilderness created by man's neglect and a retributive Nature, on the one hand, and the primeval desert on the other. But the more I continued, on subsequent visits, to study the region of Kadesh-barnea, extending to El Muweilah and westward of it, the more I became convinced that there is not only no natural boundary, but no historical boundary between the two territories either. The natural and the historical boundary between the Negeb of Israel and Sinai is Wadi el Arish, the Biblical 'River of Egypt'.

[1] Unfortunately the site is not named on any map. In Nelson Glueck's survey-map of the Negeb (1956) it is numbered 346. In *Explorations in Eastern Palestine*, II, AASOR XV (Annual of the American School of Oriental Research), (1935), pp. 120-121, Nelson Glueck writes: 'Going south-east, we came to a large, walled enclosure called Amâret Khrâsheh where a few worn Byzantine sherds were found.' From the itinerary of Nelson Glueck's expedition of 1934, from the map—unfortunately not gridded—attached to *Explorations II* and from the description of the site in this book it seems clear enough that 'Amâret Khrâsheh' is the 'Holy Mountain' of 1956.

ALONG THE NORTHERN COAST of Sinai a constant battle is being waged; a battle between the dunes invading from the sea and the men, animals and plants of a land that was once fertile. Regions which a thousand or two thousand years ago were still flourishing gardens, as the name of one of the ancient tells testifies (Tell Junein 'the garden tell', near Rafiah), have long since been buried under the dunes. Only a few isolated reminders of previous cultivation remain: an ancient well preserved by Beduin and the dwellers of the impoverished coastal settlements, pottery turned up by the archaeologist's spade, or sherds scattered among the swirling sand.

The narrow strip between sea and desert has always been a vital artery for traffic, an important military and mercantile thoroughfare. In the Bible it is referred to as 'the way of the land of the Philistines' (Exod. xiii. 17), part of the 'sea road' that connected the two great civilizations of antiquity: Babylon and Egypt. It passes through Gaza, the only port of any size on the Sinai coast and the southern coastal plain of Israel up to the first century B.C., continues to Rafiah, crosses the 'River of Egypt' (Wadi el Arish) and reaches Egypt near Qantara. The coming of Nabataean merchants into the region led to the building of at least five separate seaports between El Arish (Rhinocorura) and Gaza. The largest of them is probably identifiable as Betylium (Tell Junein and its port of Tell el Sheikh), shown on the Madeba map[1] as the 'Border of Egypt and Palestine'. Throughout the Hellenistic-Byzantine era these seaports continued to grow.

Today the region is inhabited by Arabs, whether settled or nomadic it is difficult to say, and—by the whitish-yellow sand. Beneath this sand a life lies buried, infinitely richer than that which appears above it.

FIG TREE BURIED IN SAND NEAR TELL EL SHEIKH 1

Dotted along Sinai's Mediterranean littoral were once towns and seaports. Later Arabs and Beduin settled there living in isolated huts or clustered together in small villages. They eked a scanty subsistence from the soil, particularly from date growing. They were not always successful in their constant warfare with the encroaching sand. But the sand moves on, and what has been buried by it today—like the sand-covered fruiting fig tree in the picture—to-morrow will be uncovered and free to resume its growth.

TELL JUNEIN—PROBABLY THE HELLENISTIC-ROMAN 2
BETYLIUM

Only the summit of the tell can be seen peeping out from deep layers of sand beneath which lies buried a great Hellenistic city that survived, probably into the Byzantine era. The sherds discovered here date from the Nabataean, Hellenistic, Roman and Byzantine periods. The city is in all likelihood identical with the Betylium (corresponding to the Hebrew Bethel) of the Madeba map. To-day it is a scene of complete desolation, but the name Junein ('gardens') indicates that it was once smiling countryside.

[1] One of the oldest maps extant, found in a Byzantine church in Madeba (the Biblical Medeba in Moab) in the form of a mosaic floor.

1

4

5

7

3 WORLD OF SAND

The photograph shows a group of Hebrew University students plodding along the roughly three-miles-broad sandy strip of Sinai's Mediterranean coast. From the shore the sand swirls and eddies constantly southward, reaching a height of nearly 200 feet in places, and burying ancient towns and numerous other remains.

4 ROMAN STORAGE JARS AT TELL EL SHEIKH

On the slopes of Tell el Sheikh, among date-palms half-buried in sand, some large jars, completely intact, were found. They date from the Roman period and were used for storing oil, wine or corn.

5 LETTERING ON ONE OF THE JARS

On the necks of many of the jars discovered in Tell el Sheikh are impressed Latin 'marks'. They refer either to the potter who made the jar, or to the merchant who ordered it, or to the kind of produce it was intended to hold; or else they were consignment marks. Sometimes there is lettering in red paint on the shoulders of the jar, too. The length of the measuring stick in the photograph is 20 cm. (7.9 ins).

6 TELL EL SHEIKH

Midway between Rafiah and El Arish on the Mediterranean coast of Sinai is a large tell covered with sand. This is Tell el Sheikh. The name is probably connected with the tomb of a Moslem saint, Sheikh Zuweid, which lies about three miles inland, on the edge of the sand-strip. Mainly Roman implements and sherds have been found at Tell el Sheikh. In all probability it was a seaport in Roman times and contained large warehouses. To-day there are groves of fine date-palms growing near the tell and a new well has been dug at its foot. The local inhabitants are Beduin.

7 EL ARISH CHILDREN

The El Arishía are the offspring of the many and varied peoples who came here in the course of the town's long history. Their mixed descent is reflected in their physiognomy. In one and the same street can be encountered a sloe-eyed Arab urchin with pitch-black hair—a Beduin child whose parents have chosen a settled existence—and a red- or fair-haired boy with blue or grey eyes perhaps the offspring of Crusading or Napoleonic soldiery, or of the Albanian or Bosnian troops of the Turkish Sultans, who were stationed here for long periods.

EL ARISH 8

The capital and administrative centre of Sinai. It has a population of about 10,000, mostly Moslems, who are engaged in trade and agriculture, particularly date-cultivation. They also hunt quail which are sent from here to markets in Europe.

In early times El Arish was known as Rhinocorura and according to the Madeba map was near 'the border of Egypt and Palestine'. Together with Gaza, Rafiah and Anthedon it was conquered by King Alexander Jannaeus, and formed part of the Hasmonaean kingdom. A small tell in the new town marks the site of the Roman Rhinocurura, but the site of the pre-Roman town has not yet been located. In the middle ages El Arish was a small township, about which Rabbi Meshullam, who visited it in 1481, recounts the following legend: 'We came to a place called Arish, that is Succoth, for in the language of Ishmael [sc. Arabic] "arish" means a booth [Heb. *succa*] and this is the place where our father Jacob, peace be with him, built a house' (see Gen. xxxiii. 17). The Crusaders called the place Larisa, and here King Baldwin I died in 1118. In 1799 El Arish was conquered by Napoleon in his Palestine campaign.

THE 'RIVER OF EGYPT'—WADI EL ARISH 9

Wadi el Arish is the largest of the Sinai wadis. It begins at the southern end of the plateau of Gebel et Tih and runs into the Mediterranean near the town of El Arish. Its numerous tributaries take up part of the Negeb's water and most of that of the plateau of Et Tih. In the Bible Wadi el Arish is called the 'River of Egypt'; it is the natural boundary between Israel and Sinai. Alongside it ran the ancient road from El Arish via Abu Aweigila, Jebel el Halal, Bir el Hasana (El Muweilah), Qal'at el Nakhl, and thence southwards to the Sinai mountains or west to Suez.

PART TWO   ON HOLY SOIL

We entered Sinai through a mine-field. Here and there on either side of the safe but narrow path a wrecked motor-vehicle bore witness to careless driving. I will not pretend that my companions and I in the Land-Rover felt entirely at our ease. We passed through the 'Mines' notices in silence.

After rather more than a mile of tense driving we found to our relief that we had left Wadi Sabha and were on a slightly winding road that led south to El Qusaima. From time to time the road climbed on to a saddle between two hills—mostly Egyptian observation-posts—before descending to one or the other of the small tributaries of Wadi Sabha and continuing westwards.

Suddenly one of my companions exclaimed: 'A mirage!' And indeed, shimmering on the distant horizon we saw a grove of date-palms fringing a blue sea. We jumped out of the car and stretched ourselves out on the ground to see what effect a change of perspective would have. The sea approached to within a few score yards of us—or so it seemed—only to recede far into the distance again, when we clambered back into the car.

We were still discussing the phenomenon of the mirage when the road took a sharp bend and brought us to the first mud houses of El Qusaima. We sped through the narrow street and carried on till we came to a magnificent grove of date-palms at the other end of the village. So this was El Qusaima!

It was our first stopping place on the other side of the frontier. I was surprised at the size of the village and of the grove of date-palms. I had expected to find only a few eucalyptus trees, some mud houses by a spring of brackish water, and perhaps a small frontier police post.

There is an accurate short description of the place by Woolley and Lawrence, who carried out an archaeological survey of southern Palestine in 1914:

'In Palmer's day El Qusaima seems to have been a very barren spot, but the Sinai Government, when establishing a police post here, dug out the spring, and cemented about it a basin with a long canal to take the overflow (a stream as big as Ain Qadeis) to a drinking trough and a reservoir. Below the reservoir the soldiers have made a garden in which are palm trees and fruits. The plain for a very wide space about the water-head is covered with great beds of rushes, and white with salt. The government post consists of two or three stone-built houses on little lime-stone hummocks above the spring. Beyond them on the north are some early graves. . . .'[1]

[1] C. L. Woolley and T. E. Lawrence, *The Wilderness of Zin* (ed. 1936), p. 76.

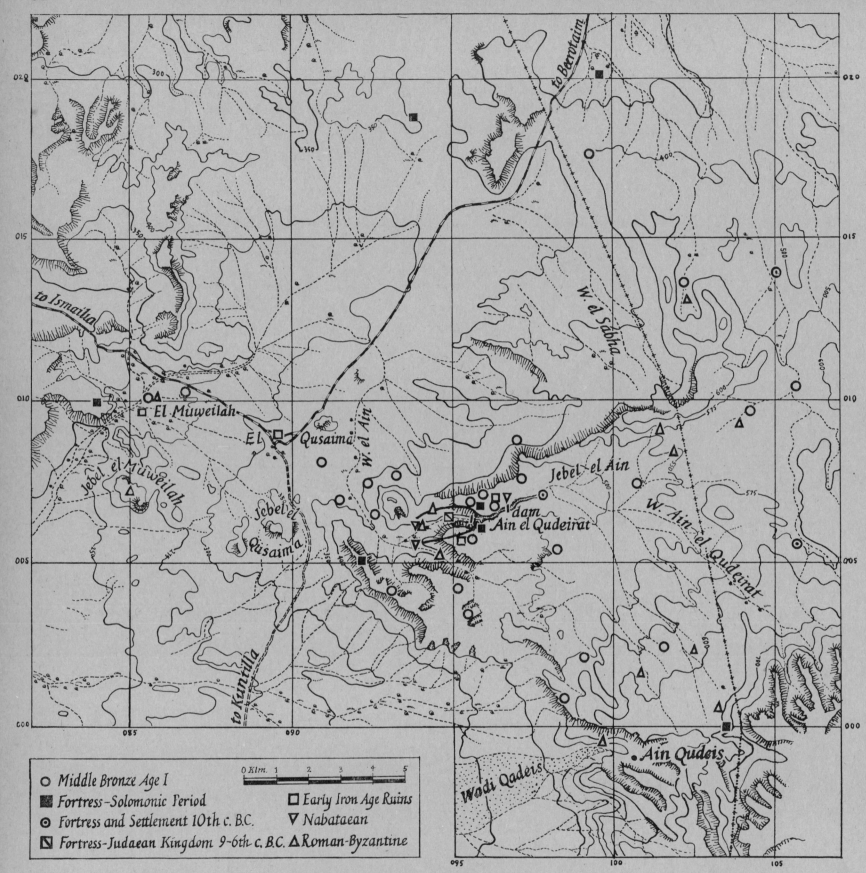

Fig. 4. Archaeological survey map of Kadesh-barnea

The grove of date-palms—hundreds of them, obviously well-tended—made a refreshing contrast to the yellow barrenness to the west. El Qusaima is surrounded by mountains and hills; to the north-east rise Jebel es Sabha and Ras Seram; to the east the great mountain ridge of Jebel el Ain presses in on the plain; and to the south rises Jebel el Qusaima, to the west of which are the mountains near El Muweilah. On the horizon it is just possible, also, to note the sharp outline of Jebel el Halal, one of the mountains considered by archaeologists to have been, possibly, the Mountain of God.

At the northern end of the grove of date-palms was a deserted Egyptian military camp: a few abandoned tents next to a large stone building. The road runs between the date-palm grove and a picturesque well and tall windmill. Next to the well were a few dingy shops and a vegetable garden bordered by shrubs.

I found this garden, humble though it was—it could not have been more than an acre in extent, at the most—peculiarly impressive. With water and toil the desert could be made to flourish. Here, near a well and next to a simple house, the inhabitants had succeeded in growing maize, egg-plants, tomatoes and peppers in neat beds. Not far from this vegetable garden stood a large building which had been severely damaged in the recent fighting—presumably the administrative headquarters of El Qusaima.

Plate 12

We spent an hour or so in El Qusaima's narrow streets and examined some of its buildings. A primitive olive press particularly aroused our interest. Olive husks lay all around on the floor. Olives? Where were the olive-trees, then? We soon found an answer to this question when we reached Wadi el Qudeirat.

My companions continued their tour of the village and the palm grove. A sentence in Woolley and Lawrence's book about 'early graves' behind the government station in El Qusaima, came into my mind. I was curious to see these remains in order to test the reliability of the book's historical identifications. Accordingly, I first examined the buildings on the hill to the north of the spring. Unfortunately, the spring itself was now under a concrete covering. By the spring was a well-house and a round water-tower built on the near slope of the hill referred to by Woolley and Lawrence. At one edge of the hill was a small group of houses. The hill, which is beyond doubt a natural one, closely resembles a tell. It is of limestone with a thin layer of sand mingled with loess. I looked for Lawrence's 'early graves'. The Egyptians had turned the flat hill into a miniature fortress and had dug trenches and gun-emplacements all around. Any early graves of course had been superseded by these later excavations, but even so, I found an appreciable quantity of sherds which may have belonged to early structures scattered among the boulders. Most of these sherds were Middle Bronze I; a few dated from the time of the Judaean kingdom (Iron Age II). The latter were crudely fashioned by hand and it was easy to see why Lawrence had assigned them to an earlier period.

I succeeded, too, in finding one structure which was more or less intact. This was a typical dwelling of the Canaanite period, resembling numerous others I had seen in the Negeb in previous years. It may be that there were once early graves on this hill, but all that could be found now were remains of a small settlement. The sherds, too, were evidently parts of Canaanite cooking pots (MB I).[1]

The first practical encounter with the views put forward by Woolley and Lawrence convinced me that it would be worth while to examine, as far as possible, the sites mentioned in their book and to collect sherds that would fix the date of these sites. In the course of our investigations in the region of Kadesh-barnea we

[1] In future I shall speak of 'Canaanite' and 'Middle Bronze Age I' interchangeably as all Canaanite remains seen by me throughout the region of Kadesh-barnea were in fact MB I.

found ourselves in complete agreement with the view expressed by Lawrence that
the whole region of El Qusaima, Ain el Qudeirat and Ain Qadeis (and also, in my
opinion, an appreciable tract on the other side of the international boundary line,
towards Beerotaim and Bir Hafir) must be held to constitute 'Kadesh-barnea', and
that this latter term must not be restricted to any one spring in the region.[1] It also
became clear to us, however, that many of Woolley and Lawrence's 'early graves'
were in fact Canaanite dwelling-places with courtyards attached, while, *per contra*,
their 'houses' were large Byzantine burial places.

In spite of my intensive searches in the immediate vicinity of Ain el Qusaima
I failed to discover any settlement dating from either the United or Divided
Monarchy. Here and there I found a few Canaanite sherds and even some which
were clearly Iron Age; but this is still a long way from proving the identification
usually made of El Qusaima with the Biblical Azmon. Admittedly, the verses in
Numbers are convincing: ' . . . (this is the land that shall fall unto you for an
inheritance, even the land of Canaan with the coasts thereof:) . . . from the south
to Kadesh-barnea, and shall go on to Hazar-addar, and pass on to Azmon: And
the border shall fetch a compass from Azmon unto the river of Egypt. . . .' (Numbers xxxiv 2, 4–5.) It is interesting to note that the Aramaic Targum Jonathan
as well as the Targum Yerushalmi have Qesem or Qisem instead of Azmon—
perhaps earlier variants of Qusaima. But the archaeological evidence provided by
our investigations, it must be repeated, does not warrant the identification of El
Qusaima with Azmon.

Without going fully into the complex problem of the identification of El Qusaima,
we may dwell on the neighbouring district of El Muweilah and the finds that were
made there. References to El Muweilah in Sinai literature are very scanty, in
spite of its being right on the Darb el Shur route and the last staging-post before
Wadi el Arish.[2] Presumably, its proximity to Ain Qadeis and Ain el Qudeirat, and,
subsequently, the importance of the junction township of El Qusaima, caused it to
be overlooked. To my mind, however, the district of El Muweilah is distinctly more
interesting, from the archaeologist's point of view, than El Quseima itself. In his
book, *The Desert of the Exodus*, the great Sinai explorer, Palmer, gives some extremely
interesting descriptions of ancient remains near the spring.[3]

Let us return to Woolley and Lawrence's book and to their description of El
Muweilah and the surrounding district:

'Ain Muweilah is a convenient starting-point in a description of the particular
features of the district in detail. It and its hills are the western limits of the good
land, and anciently it must have been the most thronged spring, since the old
inland route from Egypt runs under the cliff edge of Jebel Mushraq to the water,
and climbs up the wadi bank just beyond on its straight way to Ras Seram. On the
east side a low limestone shelf borders the valley, and upon it lie a few rude ruins
of an early period. . . . Below this limestone shelf and between its steep edge and
the flint screes of Jebel Mushraq is penned the wadi, a broad sandy bed full of
deep-rooted tamarisk trees. The drinking water is little more than a group of
shallow pools, green with slime, in the sandy bottom, which is sodden and slippery
with the heavy damp for many yards around. The place is peculiarly unattractive,
but at the same time very wet, and near it must have been a constant camping
ground. It cannot, however, have had any large or settled population, since the
possible plough-land is limited to the wadi-bed, and is sufficient only for the needs
of an inconsiderable village.'[4]

[1] ' . . . it is definitely our opinion
that only in the El Qusaima district
are to be found enough water and
greenstuffs to maintain so large a
tribe for so long and that therefore
the Wilderness of Zin and Kadesh-
barnea must be the country of Ain
el Qudeirat, El Qusaima, El
Muweilah and Ain Qadeis.' (*The
Wilderness of Zin*, p. 87). See B.
Rothenberg, "Cadès Barné" in
Bible et Terre Sainte, 1960, pp. 4-14.

[2] Robinson, *Biblical Researches*, I,
p. 190, writes: 'Further down, a
wadi enters it (Wadi el Arish) from
the left, having in it brackish
water called El Muweilah, forming
a station on the western road from
the convent to Gaza.' And this is
all he has to say about this
interesting spot.

[3] E. H. Palmer, *The Desert of the
Exodus* (Cambridge 1871), p. 355.

[4] Woolley and Lawrence, *The Wilderness of Zin*, p. 75.

All we need add to this accurate description is that since Lawrence's day some new buildings have been put up, which, however, do not concern us.

What did Lawrence find near the spring? Let us follow him and closely examine the ancient finds he describes, adding an account of a number of our own finds in the El Muweilah area.

Fig. 5 We climbed Jebel el Muweilah to obtain a view of the plain of El Qusaima and Wadi Muweilah. Lawrence says:

'The long line of stone piles on the crest of Jebel Muweilah, which made Palmer think that this must be the site of a great city, are simply memorial heaps connected with a few large ring-graves that are dotted about on the hill-top'.[1]

Why Lawrence should have foisted on to Palmer the view that precisely these strange heaps of stone were remains of a great city is difficult to understand, for he did *not* say that *these* particular remains were relics of a great city, but tended to think that they were 'connected with the worship of Baal', a view which must be dismissed of course as pure romanticism.

Lawrence writes that there were many ring-graves for which no positive dating evidence could be found owing to the absence of pottery or other objects. Nevertheless, he does assign a date to the ruins on Jebel el Muweilah by comparing them with a house ruin of the mixed rectangular and circular type which he found both on the top of Jebel el Muweilah and by the spring in the nearby wadi, where the ruin was found to be connected with an early settlement dated by pottery.

Unfortunately, Lawrence's comparison will not stand up to the evidence of the facts, including the facts of pottery. There are a number of Byzantine graves on Jebel el Muweilah, of which the rectangular pattern, as it happens, is the most characteristic. We also found a number of mixed circular and rectangular ruins, probably courtyards of a temporary settlement, and some MB I sherds. The rectangular ruin which Lawrence found at Ain el Muweilah, and which seemed conclusively to him to be of early date, is simply a Byzantine tomb of a type that is very well known in the Negeb, though it is true it was found close to a fairly extensive Canaanite settlement. Remains of an MB I settlement are found on a number of hill-tops north and south-east of the spring. On the low ridge east of the small plain of El Muweilah it is possible to distinguish 20 to 30 ruins of dwellings characteristic of the same period. Here and on the camping sites on the flat slopes round the spring, and along the road going northwards from Wadi el Muweilah to Wadi Sabha we found an appreciable number of Early Iron Age II sherds among the MB I buildings. However, I do not think there is any connexion between these Iron Age sherds discovered by us and the MB I dwellings. In all likelihood there were considerable MB I encampments around Ain el Muweilah. We did, indeed, discover a fortress of Early Iron Age type on one of the hill-tops south-east of the spring; nevertheless, during the Monarchy El Muweilah was not a sedentary settlement, but an important station on the route Hebron-Beersheba-Beerotaim (Birein)-Wadi el Arish-Bir el Hasana and onwards.[2]

Reverting to the question of the identification of Azmon, it now seems likely that the answer is to be found in the numerous early remains of El Muweilah. The large quantities of sherds dating from different periods—Bronze, Iron, Nabataean-Roman-Byzantine—discovered on the camping sites on the slopes round the spring and also along the road nearby leading north (and not passing El Qusaima at all) clearly point to a station of major importance on the main road to Wadi el Arish and onwards.

[1] Woolley and Lawrence, *The Wilderness of Zin*, p. 41.

[2] Our archaeological finds on this and other surveys showed MB I buildings and sherds continuing to Bir el Hasana and thence to the great road-junction near Parker's Monument on the Suez-Eilat road.

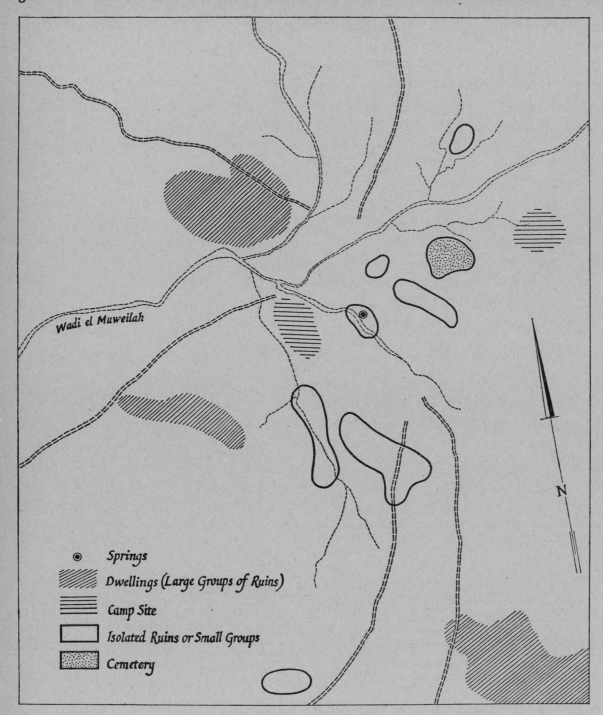

Fig. 5. Sketch plan of ancient sites at Ain Muweilah

Towards evening on the day of our visit to El Muweilah we went up to the top of Barabir el Muweilah (1,309 feet) to photograph the watershed: to the north, the plain of El Qusaima and its small but prominent hills, and, to the south, the extensive tract of land, cultivated here and there in rectangular patches all the way eastwards to Wadi Qadeis. Inevitably I was reminded of Num. xxxiv. 4, 5: '. . . . from the south to Kadesh-barnea, and shall go on to Hazar-addar, and pass on to Azmon: And the border shall fetch a compass from Azmon unto the river of Egypt. . . . ' Suddenly the dry verses began to breathe and live. We looked down and imagined the Biblical boundary, from the Negeb in the east, to Kadesh-barnea, which would have included, in addition to Ain el Qudeirat, El Qusaima, Ain Qadeis (the Biblical Hazar-addar)[1] and El Muweilah.

[1] For details of this identification see the paper in this volume: *Kadesh-barnea and Mount Sinai* by Dr Aharoni (p. 138.)

Fig. 4

Hazar-addar is the southernmost point in this region. There are patches of cultivated soil nearby. From here the border runs along Wadi Ain Qadeis and, skirting Jebel el Qusaima on the west, continues straight on to Azmon (El Muweilah) and thence to Wadi el Arish. From the mountain top we had a splendid view of the border as specified in the Biblical verses and of the greater part of the Kadesh-barnea territory and its principal water-sources.

We were all eagerly looking forward to exploring Wadi Ain el Qudeirat, and thither we now drove.[1] After a good half-mile on the Darb el Gaza (the Gaza-road) going south from El Qusaima to El Kuntilla we turned east, finding ourselves in a broad plain, along a road which had obviously borne much traffic. Occasionally a primitive terrace traversed the road and on either side we could see remains of a channel dug long ago.

The neat rows of small shrubs at the foot of the hills that hemmed in Wadi el Ain from the south gave further evidence of channelling. And now in the distance a flat-topped, cone-shaped mountain forming the background to a verdant grove of date-palms came into view. We were confident that Ain el Qudeirat: Kadesh-barnea lay ahead of us,[2] and that we were passing through territory where the Israelite hosts had encamped for a whole generation. How was it possible that we should not be able to find at least some traces of their stay here?

Hence when I saw something 'suspect' on the low hills on our right I swung the car round and hurried up the first hill (Fig. 4, co-ordinates 006.8–091.5). Here our first surprise awaited us, as a result of which we became convinced—my companions as well as myself—that it would be worth our while to come back and look for sherds, in spite of the fact that the whole area was covered with fine sand inches deep, which would render detection extremely difficult. The first thing we saw was

Plate 20

the clear remains of circular ruins covered with a thin layer of fine sand which, however, failed to dislodge my 'hunch' that they were relics of an MB I settlement. The ruins were so characteristic that I still stuck to my guns after a prolonged search had failed to yield a single sherd. I climbed to the top of the hill and saw clearly that the slopes of the adjacent hills were covered with similar remains.

On the hill-top itself I found a ruin differing in its construction from the others round about. It was in the shape of a square the sides of which measured 17 feet approximately; the walls were built with large blocks of rough stone. In spite of intensive search we failed to find a single sherd in the vicinity of this ruin. It is possible that we have here an Iron Age structure, but of course in the absence of

[1] My views in what follows on the finds in Wadi Ain el Qudeirat and the surrounding hills are based on our thorough survey of the region (see Fig. 4).

sherds we cannot be certain. My companions, however, had continued their search for sherds on the slope of this and neighbouring hills and had been able to find sherds and some flint implements; all without exception Middle Bronze Age I of the type so well known to us from the Negeb.

[2] I should explain that on this, our first trip to the region of Wadi el Qudeirat we were under the impression, formed from reading the accounts of Sinai travellers—Jarvis and others—that Kadesh-barnea was the present-day Ain el Qudeirat. Hence our excitement. It was only after exploring the whole region a number of times and studying the sources that I reached the conclusion that Kadesh-barnea must have been the name of a *fairly extensive region* embracing, *among others* the spring of Ain el Qudeirat. See also Dr Y. Aharoni's paper (pp. 122, 137, 140).

The hill on which we found this Canaanite settlement—or rather, the range of hills bordering the whole length of the wadi on which we found similar remains and sherds as we continued on our way—is situated above Wadi el Ain, not far from the spot where the wadi passes between mountains to become a narrow river-bed, and, eventually, a river of flowing water. It must not be forgotten that we were travelling 'up-stream' along the wadi, from the junction of Wadis el Risha, Sabha, el Wabsi, el Abiad and el Muweilah—all mere tributaries of the mighty Wadi el Arish itself.

Plate 11

We climbed to the top of some higher hills behind us. From here we had a fine view of the whole region; the oasis of El Qusaima—a green valley overhung by grey-white mountains, and the bed of Wadi el Ain winding between the peaks to the east. The cone-shaped mountain we had seen ahead of us before, now turned out to be—as a glance at the map showed us—one of the extremities of Jebel el Ain.

Plate 20

At the other side of the wadi, too, on one of the foothills, we saw relics of a Canaanite settlement (co-ordinates 092.4–007.4), and on a later trip we found further Canaanite ruins both to the north and east of this settlement (co-ordinates 092.6–005.5 and 093.3–007.3).

We drove on along the wide road that runs alongside Wadi el Ain, first on its right bank, then through the middle, and later on its left. The steep hills, about 300 feet high, of Jebel el Ain border it on both sides.[1]

The road went slightly uphill, with shrubs and olive trees on either side, until about half-way along its length the wadi narrowed. It is at this spot that a small but prominent 'tell'[2] came into view; we had reached the famous site of the fortress dating from the Hebrew monarchy mentioned in most text-books of Palestinian archaeology as being the classic example of an Israelite fortress.

Plate 10

Plate 15

The tell stood out clearly, almost white in contrast to the dun colouring of the Wadi. Even apart from this, its structure and position in the wadi showed it to be a mound that was wholly artificial to its foundations in the depths of the wadi. Leaving the neglected orchard at the foot of the tell we clambered a few yards up the side to the top, which was almost flat. Of Lawrence's excavations not a trace remained. Only at the ends was there projecting masonry, perhaps remains of the corner watch-towers, and the wall-foundations. We began to look for sherds, for we were anxious to find out for ourselves when the fortress was built. We spent a long time searching. Eventually all our sherds were heaped in the middle of the tell and we sat around examining them one by one—all Iron Age II, dating from the time of the Kingdom of Judah. There were sherds such as have been found in Northern Palestine as well as those peculiar to the fortifications of the Negeb. All dated from the same period: 8th to 6th centuries B.C.; perhaps a little earlier. We were of course disappointed at finding nothing that ante-dated this period. Only a poor consolation was offered by some sherds which we found dating from the 'Persian' period (the time of the return of the exiles from Babylon), from which we were able to learn a new historical fact; namely, that after the Babylonian Exile Jews returned to, and settled in, this region.

[1] On the map only the northern heights are called 'Jebel el Ain', but I shall refer to those on the southern bank as Jebel el Ain too. In point of fact the mountain range round Ain el Qudeirat forms a broad, lofty plateau stretching south from the Jebel el Ain marked on the map to Ain Qadeis. A number of wadis—Wadi Ain el Qudeirat, Wadi Umm Hushib and various tributaries—have their source on this plateau and in their westward flow cut deep ravines in the great range of Jebel el Ain.

In the large olive grove on the northern side of the valley of Ain el Qudeirat, where the plain ends and the narrow wadi starts, we found a large number of Byzantine sherds, showing that this was the main area of settlement in the Byzantine period. We found no buildings that were standing, but here and there we could discover a heap of stones, relics of a crumbling wall, and meagre remains of structural foundations. On a later expedition, led by Dr Aharoni, we left the hill-top, after following the great wall—to be discussed later—and searched for sherds at this spot. We succeeded in finding a number of Nabataean sherds on a tract of ground behind the trees, proving that a considerable Nabataean settlement once existed there. Such sherds had not previously been found in any quantity, although a number of expeditions and survey-groups looking for sherds had been there.

[2] The Arabic name for an artificial mound or hillock.

Plate 88

We also went up Jebel el Ain on the north side of the wadi. Here, just above the spring, we found many clear remains of the Middle Bronze I period. On subsequent trips we walked along the whole northern neck of land up to the international boundary line and found numerous remains of various periods, chiefly Middle

Plate 19

Bronze Age.[1] On the plateau too, on the other side of the wadi leading to Ain Qadeis, were Middle Bronze Age remains, and here we also found a number of Iron Age structures, as well as flint implements in profusion, mostly Palaeolithic, though some were Middle Bronze Age and some, perhaps, Neolithic. On the plateau there were many relics of Byzantine agriculture: dwellings, dams, irrigation canals and superbly planned terraces, with signs of flourishing vegetation still evident. Here and there we found evidence of recent Beduin cultivation among these ancient terraces.

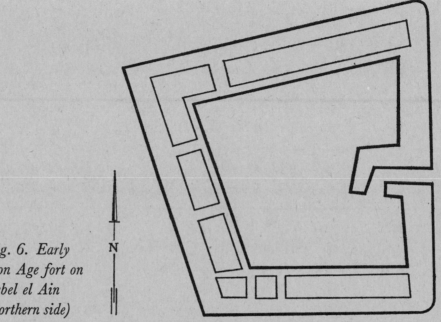

Fig. 6. Early Iron Age fort on Jebel el Ain (northern side)

N

In the days of the Hebrew monarchy there was a simple but well-organized system of defence here. The tell in the middle of the wadi was not a look-out post, but a rallying-point from which the spring could be defended. A number of watch-towers were built on neighbouring hills, enabling the slightest movement in the distance to be detected. On the ridge of the hills south-west of Wadi el Ain, before it (the wadi) takes a sharp turn to the east (Fig. 4, co-ordinates 005.1–094.2) stood a square watch-tower; small, but well built of unhewn stone. An appreciable quantity of sherds dating from the monarchy was found here. This structure is an exact replica in style and size—about 13 feet square—of another of the same date found at the mouth of the wadi (Fig. 4, co-ordinates 007.2–098) and guarding the entrance to it at the point where several of its tributaries coming from the east intersect. A similar tower, though smaller, stands at the south end of the wadi, above the spring, but it is in such a poor state of preservation that it is difficult to give its precise dimensions.[2]

Exactly opposite this smaller tower is an Iron Age fortress which is still the subject of archaeological controversy. This structure is much simpler than the fortress on the tell in the wadi, but the corners are of fairly solid construction.[3] The sherds discovered here are of the crude Iron Age type found in the Negeb and Sinai, resembling those found by the fortress of Ain Qadeis.

One striking fact emerged after we had discovered and examined a number of Middle Bronze Age I remains in this region; a fact which may help to elucidate a number of archaeological and historical problems connected with Kadesh-barnea:

[1] See Fig. 4, showing the exact location of the various sites, with their identifications, which we investigated on our explorations of the region.

[2] This watch-tower had been previously discovered, it seems, by Nelson Glueck. See AASOR XV (1935), p. 119 (Site 251).

[3] See Y. Aharoni (p. 125). The plan sketched in Fig. 6 is based on aerial photography.

we cannot point to any particular centre of Canaanite settlement in the region and it is unlikely that any city-like centre ever existed. In Kadesh-barnea we do indeed find small and medium-sized groupings of Canaanite remains, all of a pattern similar to that known to us from the Negeb, but we cannot say that any of these constituted a 'centre'.[1] The great majority of the remains convey the impression of 'family settlements'. Their wide dispersal over the whole area of the major springs—such as those of El Qudeirat and El Muweilah—bears a close resemblance to the way in which the Beduin tribes live dispersed in their goatskin tents.

It is true there are two larger-than-single-family groupings on the hill-sides south-west of Wadi el Ain. In addition, there is a fairly large settlement on a (purposely?) concealed site on the hill-top by the southern bank of Wadi Umm Hushib (Fig. 4, co-ordinates 004–096). None of these constitute a 'centre', however. Evidently the dwelling pattern of the Canaanites, Amorites and Amelekites in the region bore an astonishing resemblance to that of semi-nomads in all ages down to our own.

Of special interest, perhaps, is the fact that the land near the spring, particularly the land bounded by the great wall of Wadi Ain Qudeirat, was never settled on at any time (except for the site of the central Iron Age fortress in the wadi near the spring). Was this fortuitous? Or was the malaria prevailing in the wadi even in those days sufficient reason to get as far away as possible from the spring in the evenings?

A little west of the spring, where a mysterious wall we shall discuss presently   Plate 17
descends from the hill-side into the valley, there is a new dam built on the initiative of Major Jarvis, a former governor of Sinai. The dam, about 10 feet high, is surrounded by olive trees, date-palms, fine tall plum trees, clumps of reeds and other vegetation. In spite of this attractive décor the new dam strikes a jarring note. It is built on the foundations of an ancient dam which gathered up the waters of the spring and conducted them, in part, to a big reservoir on the southern slope of Wadi el Ain. The new construction, all polished white limestone, seems incongruous. Jarvis himself describes in his book, *Desert and Delta*, how he traced the ancient reservoir and dam and supervised their repair.

But in addition to these, the most interesting feature of Wadi el Ain is the mysterious wall. This is described with his customary accuracy by Lawrence, who, however, is able to propound only a tentative solution to the mystery:

'Starting above this Byzantine village, and running eastward along the hill-top,   Plate 10
there is one of the long and puzzling walls which, like those elsewhere in the Negeb, appear to start and go on and end so aimlessly. It is a wall of dry stone, perhaps three-quarters of a mile long in all, and still perfectly preserved. It has been piled up very carelessly, from two to three feet thick, and from three to five feet high. It runs reasonably directly along the hill, never at the crest, but always a little way down the valley slope; it crosses gullies on the hill-side, without varying its height or taking any regard of them; in one place it is broken by plain openings, flanked internally by a square enclosure, a few feet each way, like a pound, or a temporary shelter. Its purpose is mysterious. Being on the downward slope of the hill it would not keep anyone out, and, besides, it runs only from one side-wadi to another, and so would not really protect anything. It cannot be meant to keep human beings enclosed, for any child that could crawl would overpass it; nor would it pen any sheep or goat. The only Arab animal that would find such an

[1] See Plate 20 and Fig. 9, p. 62.

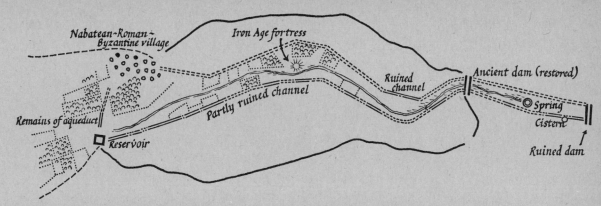

Fig. 7. Sketch plan of the Nabataean system of irrigation in Wadi el Ain

erection impassable would be a camel, and, perhaps, the wall is the monument of some tribe's exasperation in herding camels. The beasts have a perverse habit of wandering up a steep hill-side and becoming incurably lost, and this wall, if supported by fences across the valley at its two ends, would prevent their escape entirely. The present Qudeirat tribe disclaim all responsibility for the work; but they are comparative newcomers in the district.'[1]

I examined the wall on several occasions. The first time I was able to see only the ends that went down into the valley. The lack of any apparent purpose in a wall descending straight from the hill-side to end abruptly in the wadi baffled me completely. On the second occasion we inspected the great reservoir, and, taking this as our starting point, we followed the southern wall along its whole length until its sudden termination near the dam at the head of the wadi. This time we found a number of ruins near the wall. Some of these dated from the Middle Bronze Age, the rest were Iron Age (we also found Iron Age sherds), but we remained quite unable to account for the wall itself.[2] I found myself in Wadi el Ain again later with a group of Dr Aharoni's Hebrew University students. This time we trailed the northern wall, starting near the dam and continuing along Jebel el Ain until the descent of the wall at the 'Byzantine village'—in point of fact a large Nabataean settlement. At this point the wall ends for no apparent reason, giving the impression that it had been demolished from here onwards.

We examined the openings in the wall so carefully described by Lawrence. These were found to be later additions, Byzantine according to the evidence of the sherds. In summarizing his conclusions Dr Aharoni contends that the archaeological evidence enables us to affirm confidently that the wall is pre-Byzantine. He is inclined to assign its construction to the time of the monarchy (Iron Age II), and he declares its purpose was to 'indicate and set bounds to the sacred place'.[3] My own views on the purpose served by the wall differ from Dr Aharoni's.

Above the main spring is a moist area indicating that in all probability one or more secondary springs rose from the rocks here too. The most significant feature, however, is that beyond the whole of this moist area, further up the wadi and quite a fair distance from the main spring, are remains of a ruined dam rising to about six feet in height, partly covered by silt. An abundance of shrubs and other plants around the dam show that in winter the area receives a considerable quantity of water. Near the dam is the opening of a water-cistern. A rock-cut channel leads from the dam, passing close to the spring but maintaining a constant height above it, along the south side of the wadi. The spring itself flows deep down in the valley,

[1] C. L. Woolley and T. E. Lawrence, *The Wilderness of Zin*, pp. 80-81.

Plate 16

[2] See survey-map of Kadesh-barnea region, p. 34.

[3] See *Kadesh-barnea and Mount Sinai*, p. 139 ff. of this volume.

both through an iron pipe till it reaches the reservoir at the mouth of the wadi, and as a muddy rivulet to the new dam, near which remains of another, ancient dam can still be clearly seen. I was unable to ascertain whether the waters of this second ancient dam flowed through the rock-cut channel leading from the first higher up the wadi, or whether they passed through a ruined channel the remains of which were visible here and there on the north side of the wadi. The southern channel was more or less well preserved, and its course could be traced to the great reservoir in the valley opposite the village. Only a few remains of the northern channel have been preserved, however; and all we can say is that at one time there was a channel leading from the ancient, subsequently restored, dam to the Nabataean village.

It is important to bear in mind that this latter dam is situated in the narrowest part of the valley, at a spot where it bends sharply, and a hill on the south side projects into the wadi to form a gorge. The mysterious wall, be it noted, runs down from both sides of the valley to this very spot. My first impression, which had undergone no modification at the conclusion of our survey, was that the walls had diverted the rainwater from the surrounding hills to this dam. One has only to look at aerial photographs and see the small but deep gullies leading from the ridges to the wadi to feel that this must have been so. The wall evidently served a dual purpose: to prevent the channels that ran along the slopes below from being blocked up with detritus, and to divert the rainwaters both eastwards to the dam and westwards to the great reservoir and the large Nabataean settlement. I believe in chance, but I find it hard to believe that the four ends of the wall just 'happened' to be built in the heart of a well-planned system of irrigation in the bed of the valley.   Fig. 7

Let us now return to the problem of the dam at the head of the wadi. Why was it necessary to construct it at this spot where there were no springs of water which could fill it? To answer this question we must note carefully where the large spring and the small hidden springs in the bed of the valley were situated. All these springs lay in a deep, narrow gully, and there can be no doubt that on more than one occasion their very existence was endangered by spate-borne earth and boulders coming down from the top of the valley slopes. In all likelihood the dam was built primarily to prevent the springs from being wrecked by flood damage, but with the subsidiary purpose of holding the waters in check and conducting them to the reservoir. The fact that when Jarvis was governor, the government saw no reason to restore the dam at the head of the valley, though it did restore the rest of the valley's irrigation system, can be accounted for by the main spring already being well protected by strong concrete walls, a thick roof and the iron pipes through which it flowed.

From the second, restored, dam, let us continue our way, passing water-channels on both sides of the valley, along the wadi. We pass the hill of the fortress, which has no connexion with the valley's irrigation system—the brook flowing in the valley at the foot of the hill provided plentiful water for the garrison. Here there are some exceptionally fine cultivated fields bearing traces of recent tilth. The Arabs had recently planted here among the older trees, in enclosed fields at the foot of the fortress, olives, apricots and figs—I even noticed a lemon-tree and some vines. A little farther up the valley wheat or barley seems to have been grown, thanks to the plentiful water supply available.

The area under cultivation increases as the valley opens out. The water channel on the southern side of the wadi remains at the same height. This channel appears to be ascending all the time, but this is an optical illusion, due to the fact that the narrow wadi-bed follows a downward slope, while the channel keeps on the level all the time. Near the great square reservoir, surrounded by plum and pine trees, and near a large orchard, on a slope about 22 feet above the wadi-bed, the channel stops. Towards the end we found it difficult to make out traces of the ancient conduit that once ran on the north side of the wadi where today we see a new narrow, concreted water-channel, which has obliterated it. However, we may safely assume that the ancient conduit, too, which was solidly built of hewn blocks of stone, ran the whole length of the wadi, which it served to irrigate. It may even have brought water to the Nabataean-Byzantine village near the beginning of the outer foothills.

From the site of the Nabataean village to the reservoir remains of an aqueduct built of hewn stone, crossing the wadi-bed in a south-northerly line, can be seen. Presumably this was used to bring drinking water from the reservoir to the inhabitants of the village.

It remains only to describe the reservoir itself. It is a remarkably fine, four square structure, about 27 feet each way, and as far as could be ascertained about 10 feet deep. It is built of great blocks of hewn stone, but with later additions in parts; the brim, in particular, has been repaired and re-rendered, evidently by Jarvis. The style of construction resembles that of some of the structures I have examined in the Negeb. It differs greatly from the Byzantine masonry in the region; the courses are laid more precisely and the stone hewn more finely. Lawrence, who was the first to examine the reservoir,[1] describes it as Byzantine, but he describes the great Nabataean settlement nearby as Byzantine, too. However, there can be no doubt that with the revised dating of the settlement we must redate Lawrence's Byzantine reservoir to the Nabataean era. The water-supply system in Wadi el Qudeirat was constructed in accordance with a carefully considered plan and based on sound hydro-engineering principles. This is shown by the fact that the reservoir was built about 22 feet above the wadi-bed and not in the middle of it. Moreover, the great channel from the head of the valley extends to this spot, and the wall runs down in a direct line to it. In my view there were a number of good reasons for building the reservoir above the level of the stream, of which the chief two were: [1] its construction fairly high up would have enabled the fields to be irrigated for a considerable distance around by force of gravity alone, and [2] its construction on the level of the wadi-bed would have meant a catastrophe with the advent of winter floods or the sand-storms prevalent in the region.

In the evening of our first day's exploration of Kadesh-barnea we stood on the northern slopes of Jebel el Ain and surveyed to the west the wadi twisting and turning below us and the outstretched plain of El Qusaima, veiled in a faint haze by the rays of the setting sun. Here, in this broad plain of long dark shadows and golden-gleaming hillocks the Children of Israel encamped for a whole generation; from here the spies set forth on their way across the Negeb mountains to reconnoitre the Land of Canaan. Kadesh-barnea, comprising the region of Ain el Qudeirat, Ain Qadeis, El Qusaima and El Muweilah, was the springboard for the invasion of Canaan and the crucible in which the eternal faith of an eternal nation was put to the cruel test of the wilderness. Here Moses wrestled for the destiny of his people and here his own destiny was decided.

[1] C. L. Woolley and T. E. Lawrence, *The Wilderness of Zin*, pp. 78 ff.

KADESH-BARNEA was one of the main staging-posts on the Israelites' trek to the Promised Land.

'. . . and the children of Israel went out with an high hand' (Exod. xiv. 8). But the hardships of the journey, the barren wilderness, the marauding desert tribes, soon led to 'Massah, and Meribah, because of the chiding of the children of Israel' (Exod. xvii. 7). 'And when we departed from Horeb, we went through all that great and terrible wilderness, which ye saw by the way of the mountain of the Amorites, as the LORD our God commanded us; and we came to Kadesh-barnea' (Deut. i. 19). Kadesh became the centre from which the conquest of Canaan was planned. From here the spies set out to reconnoitre the Promised Land. Here, too, the 'generation of the wilderness' rebelled against the commandment of Moses and refused to go forth to the conquest. 'So ye abode in Kadesh many days, according unto the days that ye abode there' (Deut. i. 46).

The springs of Kadesh-barnea were regarded as holy in very ancient times. To the nomadic desert tribes these waters gushing forth in the heart of the wilderness seemed symbolic; hence the name: Kadesh ('holy'). From the earliest times men have built their settlements around springs of water. In the time of the Patriarchs, Kadesh had a comparatively large population. Many families pitched their tents, built their farmsteads and cultivated the soil in the valley of Kadesh-barnea. They did not dwell by the holy stream itself, however, and remains of ancient settlements have been found only on the escarpments encompassing it.

The Israelites maintained the tradition of holiness with which the area was invested and 'the waters of Meribah-Kadesh' saw the divine effulgence: 'The LORD came from Sinai, and rose up from Seir unto them: he shined forth from mount Paran, and he came with ten thousands of saints: from his right hand went a fiery law for them' (Deut. xxxiii. 2).

The life-giving waters of Kadesh were a source of strife among the nomadic desert tribes, as we may gather from the reference in Gen. xiv. 7. to 'En Mishpat (the well of judgement) which is Kadesh'. But Moses and Aaron, too, strove with God at this spot, Moses striking the rock, instead of speaking to it, as God had commanded him. And Kadesh, where God sentenced Moses and Aaron: 'Ye shall not bring this congregation into the land which I have given them,' received a new name: 'This is the water of Meribah; because the children of Israel strove with the LORD, and he was sanctified in them' (Num. xx. 13).

WADI EL AIN 10

General view, taken from Jebel el Ain (north side). Part of the wall encircling the wadi can be seen, as well as the fortress of Ain el Qudeirat (next to the clump of trees centre) and the plain with its olive groves. The Nabataean village is right, and the great reservoir left, of the grove in the background.

13

14

16

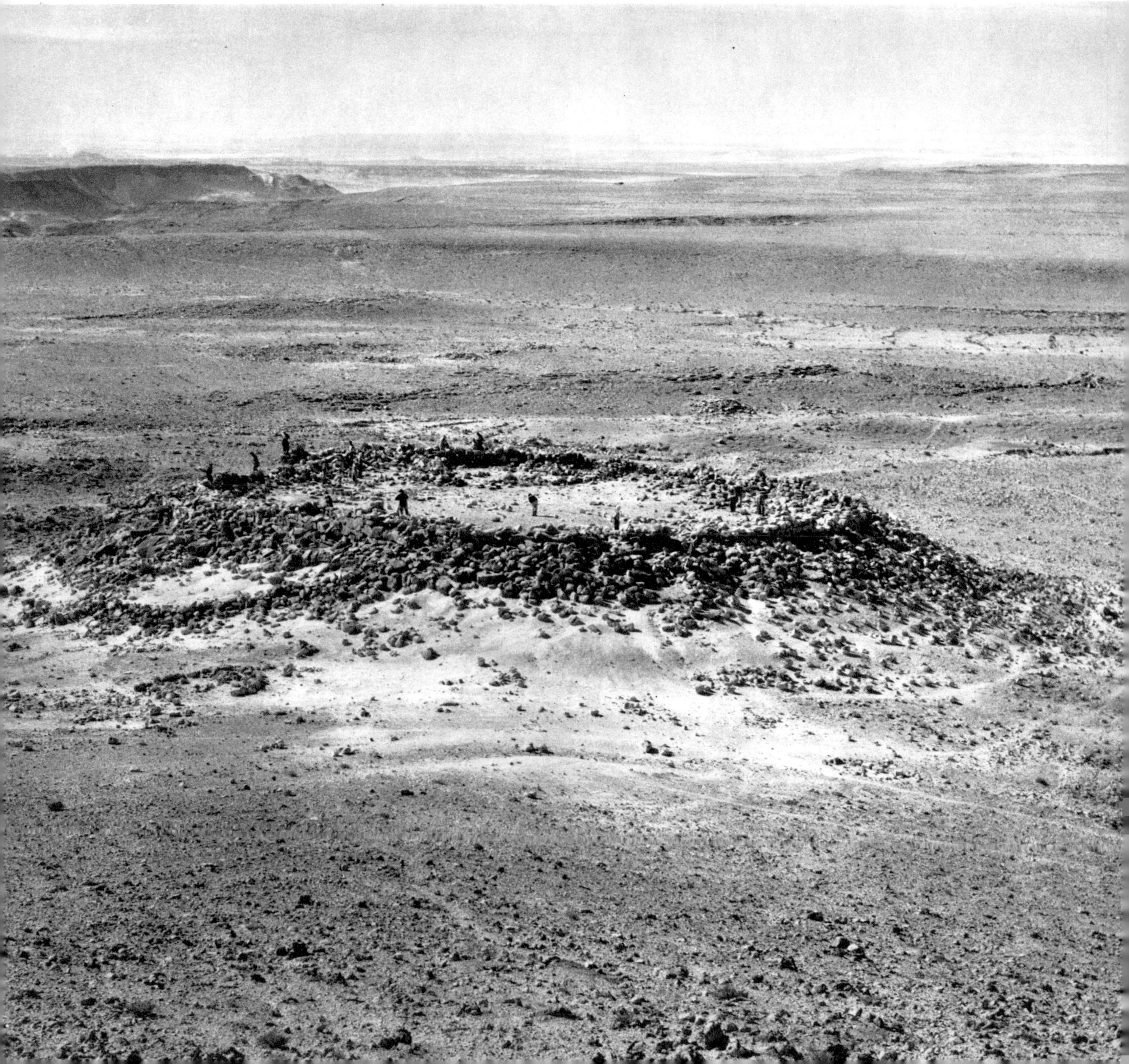

18

19

20

11 AIN EL QUDEIRAT

Wadi el Ain has the most copious spring in the whole of the Negeb and Sinai: Ain el Qudeirat, first identified by Woolley and Lawrence as the Biblical Kadesh-barnea. Although at the present day the stream has been compressed within banks of concrete, and most of its water directed into an iron pipe-line running the length of Wadi el Ain, there is still a small brook running through the wadi and transforming it into a green plot in the barren Sinai desert.

12 OLIVE PRESS IN EL QUSAIMA

In one of the houses in the village of El Qusaima was found a communal olive press, very similar to those described in the Mishna. In the picture can be seen the two heavy stone rollers which move on a solid base about seven feet in diameter. The rollers are turned by a camel or pair of asses.

The process of extracting oil with the aid of revolving apparatus was known in Hellenistic times and has been described in detail by Cato and Pliny. In Biblical times it seems that oil was extracted with the aid of millstones similar to those used for grinding corn.

13 BYZANTINE VILLAGE NEAR AIN QADEIS

This lies on the broad plateau of Jebel el Ain, about two miles from Ain Qadeis. The villagers cultivated a large stretch of land irrigated by artificial canals. They built terraces and lived in solid houses of stone. In the lower half of the picture remains of dwelling-houses and some of the large terraces can be seen. In the centre can be seen the long stone perimeter fence enclosing the whole area under cultivation. The plots between the terraces are still cultivated by the Beduin.

14 THE NABATAEAN DAM IN WADI EL AIN

This dam was built above the spring to protect its waters. The solid construction of the dam is apparent even in the present ruins. The remains of the channel dug in the rock of the wadi-bed can also be seen (right of the dam).

15 REMAINS OF FORTRESS DATING FROM THE KINGS OF JUDAH, NEAR THE SPRING

In the neck of Wadi el Ain is a small tell on top of which is a fortress dating from the Hebrew monarchy. The ground plan of this fortress, as published by T. E. Lawrence, has become the standard example of an Israelite fortress. In the picture the walls of the fortress can be clearly traced. Lawrence gives the dimensions of the tell as 200 feet long and 120 feet broad. Most of the tell's sherds belong to Iron Age II (8th to 6th centuries), but some dating from the Return to Zion (Persian period) have also been found.

In the photograph the wall on Jebel el Ain surrounding a great part of the wadi can also be clearly seen (see note on Plate 17).

THE FORTRESS OVERLOOKING AIN QADEIS, DATING 16
FROM THE EARLY PERIOD OF THE MONARCHY

Discovered by Dr Y. Aharoni. The fortress consists of a casemate wall. Sherds
found on the site point to the fortress being of Davidic or Solomonic construction
(10th century or earlier). This is one of the largest and strongest of the Early Iron
Age fortifications in the Negeb discovered so far, and would seem to be the Biblical
Hazar-addar (survey-map p. 34, co-ordinates: 103.4–000.2).

THE MYSTERIOUS WALL ROUND WADI EL AIN 17

A wall of boulders, about 3 feet thick and 5 feet high, runs from both banks of
the wadi up to Jebel el Ain, where it runs along the ridge of the hill for about three-
quarters of a mile and then ends up in the narrowest part of the wadi near an
ancient reservoir still in use. The wall encircles the part of the wadi in which the
tell with its Israelite fortress lies. The precise significance or function of the wall is
difficult to ascertain and is still a matter of controversy. It is discussed by Y. Aharoni and B. Rothenberg on pages 138–140 and 42–44 respectively.

A CORNER OF THE OUTER WALL OF THE FORTRESS 18
SHOWN IN PLATE 16

A good example of building construction in the Israelite period. The large, roughly-
hewn blocks of stone are laid 'stretcher' and 'header' alternating.

REMAINS OF HOUSE, MIDDLE CANAANITE PERIOD (MB I) 19
ON JEBEL EL AIN

On the ridge of the hill on both sides of the wadi, numerous remains were found,
both of graves and of dwellings, dating from the Patriarchal period (see survey-map
of Kadesh-barnea, p. 34). The houses of the period were built, mainly on a
circular plan, of rough stone. In many cases a large upright stone stands inside
the dwelling close to the wall. The impress of an oven or fireplace can often be
discerned in the houses or the courtyards attached to them.

REMAINS OF SETTLEMENT DATING FROM EARLY 20
PATRIARCHAL TIMES, WADI EL AIN

On the slopes of the low hills enclosing Wadi el Ain, not far from El Qusaima
remains of settlements dating from the beginning of the Patriarchal period were
discovered. This is the first time such remains have ever been discovered in Sinai
(Survey-map, p. 34, reference: 091.5–006.8). The greater part of the buildings are
no longer preserved, but the foundations are intact. The sherds discovered near
the ruins clearly belong to Middle Bronze Age I.

PART THREE   IN THE FOOTSTEPS OF THE PILGRIMS

Plate 8

We set out early the next morning with high hopes but no particular plans, from El Arish. We intended eventually to reach the 'oil city' of Ras el Sudr in the Gulf of Suez and on the way to get to know the desert of Et Tih, the great central plateau of Sinai.

Immediately we found ourselves driving on a first-class road going south across a broad plain along the mighty Wadi el Arish (the Biblical 'River of Egypt'). Here and there the flat bright yellow landscape was broken up by ranges of low hills. The general impression was one of spaciousness and of dazzling sunshine.

Plate 9

This was the true frontier of Sinai. Nature itself seemed to proclaim that the Wadi was the dividing line between the desert and the fertile land. On our left we passed cultivated fields interspersed among the sand dunes and on the sides of the flat hills, while to our right the desert scrub struggled for a pitiful existence in rocky gullies, and the sand hummocks were bare.

The next lap of our journey, to Bir el Hasana, can be described briefly. Leaving the 'River of Egypt' behind us we drove at full speed through the sandy, blinding Sinai wilderness. The road passed through a plain strewn with desert-scrub, pebble and scree; in the distance we could see Jebel el Halal on one side and Jebel el Maghara on the other.

Plate 21

After about twenty miles the road hugs the foot of Jebel Libni, a mountain criss-crossed with gullies from top to bottom. We now found ourselves for the first time in the flinty black-and-white plain, the *hamada*, which was to be the monotonous, unvarying landscape of our subsequent journey through the wilderness of Et Tih.

Crossing the Abu Aweigila–Ismailia road, we continued south. Once more we found ourselves on an open plain of shifting sand and low scrub. Here and there we passed a stretch of dried-up, sun-baked winter mud, with gaping rents and holes in it, like a brick field. Jebel el Halal now came into full view, rising suddenly and majestically in the heart of the plain to its height of approximately 3,000 feet.

Plate 27

As we approached Bir el Hasana, the road entered the broad bed of Wadi el Hasana, which at this spot pursues a winding course and then splits up into a number of flat tributaries. The landscape consisted of hummocks of sand, shingle and occasionally a snow-white hill. After driving another mile or so we saw a grove and a few buildings some way ahead. We made a brief halt to consult the map and to photograph Bir el Hasana from the distance. I climbed up a hill by the roadside, a few hundred yards north of the Hasana well, and found some early remains. It was difficult to ascertain the precise nature of these heaps of stones in their present state. They reminded me of the circular Middle Bronze Age structures of the Negeb and Kadesh-barnea; but the few sherds we were able to find, after much labour, in the shifting sand that covers everything here to a depth of eight to twelve inches, gave no clue to a positive identification. We combed the sand with our bare hands, but in vain. All one could say was that both masonry and sherds suggested the Middle Bronze I period, but it was impossible to be sure. We found some compensation, however, in an appreciable quantity of flint implements we collected, all of Upper Palaeolithic or Late Middle Palaeolithic type.

Bir el Hasana is a main road-junction on the Et Tih plateau, and the end of the good road leading south from El Arish. From here one road forks south-west to the road-junction at Parker's Monument—which we were later to visit—and continues via the Mitla pass to Suez. The other road, practically impassable, runs straight south to Qal'at el Nakhl on the Pilgrim's Way (Darb el Haj). Hasana itself consists of a small green grove of tamarisk and palm sited against a background of white limestone hills. On all sides of it, the desolate plain stretches away. The hills on the horizon do nothing to soften the impression of barrenness. Round the well (which has recently been reconstructed) are a few scattered buildings—a government block, an hotel, the remains of a disused Khan and police-station.

We searched unsuccessfully for early remains in the vicinity of the well and on the nearby hills. All we could find were a few implements, such as are scattered all over the plateau of Et Tih, the overwhelming majority being of the Upper Palaeolithic type.[1]

I was anxious to visit Jebel el Halal, as I was inclined to the view that this was the Biblical Mount Sinai, the Mountain of God. After a brief pause at Hasana, we resumed our journey with high hopes, determined to make a thorough inspection of the Jebel el Halal area. The mountain itself gained in impressiveness as we drew nearer to it. After driving for an hour or so we passed a white cone-shaped hill that stood out curiously in the flat plain; in the distance we descried a ruined cistern that had been sunk at the foot of the hill.

We by-passed a sandy wadi that crossed the road and reached a water cistern, probably ancient, of fine workmanship. The plain hereabouts showed signs of cultivation, particularly in the flat offshoot-wadis of Wadi el Arish.[2]

Numerous low terraces and Byzantine sherds testified to a once-busy hum of life in the region of the mountain. From here the road draws closer to the mountain, only to leave it farther in the distance later, until suddenly we found ourselves at the ruins of an old house, not far from which, in a small canyon carved out of the limestone of the mountain, was Bir el Hadeira.

We set out to look for early remains. By the roadside, not far from the entrance to the depression, we found a large MB I settlement, as well as an abundance of ruins on the gently-sloping hill-sides and along the small wadis that run down from the mountain top towards the entrance to the depression. Here many of the sherds we found were Arab and no doubt some of the stone circles we saw were built by Beduin also. But many circular stone structures on the southern and northern slopes of the depression and on the whitish slopes north of Bir el Hadeira were MB I, as was clear both from the style of construction and from the sherds we collected.

In the depression, particularly at the foot of the steep slopes of the Jebel, we found, in addition to many MB I remains, a large number of wells, some with

[1] Cf. C. T. Currelly's description of the flint implements discovered by him about fifty years ago: 'Strewn over this are thousands of flakes and implements from Palaeolithic times. The flint seems to be good, and there are quantities of large pieces; yet the implements are all small and of decidedly poor workmanship. The majority have the orange patina well known on Libyan flints. One or two flints were of the regular celt pattern, but the majority were small scrapers.' In W. M. Flinders Petrie, *Researches in Sinai*, 1906, p. 267.

[2] I flew south-east over this region on another occasion. At this spot Wadi el Arish 'swallows' Wadi Jeraya and its numerous feeders and from the air it was possible to make out thousands of terraces along the whole length of the great watercourse. Near the spot whence Wadi Jeraya flows north-west is the frontier post of Kuntillet Jeraya, plentifully supplied with water. Unfortunately I was not able to examine this region on the ground, but even from the air it was possible to detect the early remains north of the spring. The Arabic word *Jeraya*, too, suggests the existence of an early settlement here.

water. I counted these and made them fifteen all told, in addition to the one by the roadside.

Undoubtedly the depression of Jebel el Halal is full of archaeological interest. Unfortunately the limited time at our disposal made it impossible for us to see and examine more than a fraction of the material available. There are many ancient remains, and early sherds, mostly Canaanite. Some sherds may be Iron Age (particularly the crude kind of the type found all over the Negeb), others Nabataean and Roman-Byzantine.

We returned to Bir el Hasana. Next morning we set out again on the road to Suez. Our first objective was Sudr el Heitan, where the road from Bir el Hasana links up with the Pilgrim's Way.

Plates 21, 27

Wadi el Hasana, which runs parallel to the road for about ten miles from Bir el Hasana, is a *hamada* landscape in which the small pieces of black flinty rock chequering the white ground present a curious natural spectacle.

Suddenly a chain of low hills, all of uniform height, came into view gleaming in the strong sunlight. We left the road and drove right down into the bottom of the wadi. It was completely bare, both the bed and walls being of white limestone; the walls, however, were topped with a layer of at least two yards of good loess soil. They looked like slices of cream cake cut on the slant. From here Jebel Ekhtifah, a mountain a mile-and-a-quarter to a mile-and-three-quarters long, can be clearly seen, its dark colouring standing out in the surrounding glare. It is a basalt mountain, 'the richest source of basalt in the desert'.[1]

Once more we took to the road, which continued for many miles across the same unchanging gullies and gravel plain. And now the plateau of Et Tih was rising to a thousand feet or more above sea-level, and more and more lofty peaks were coming into view. To the north-west a high imposing mountain-range, the Jebel Yeleg,[2] blocked out the horizon.

After driving another twenty miles or so we reached the environs of Bir el Themada, on the northern bank of Wadi el Bruq, one of the main southern tributaries of Wadi el Arish. Wadi el Bruq opens out, at the spot where the road crosses it, into a great plain of sand and gravel nearly seven miles long and three miles wide. Far off to the south, more mountains could be descried on the horizon.

We stopped about half-a-mile from the well (of Bir Themada) and on the banks of the wadi nearby found some worked flints of medium size and not of particularly fine workmanship. We collected a number of scrapers and gouges typologically identical with those we had found both on Jebel el Ain and near Bir el Hasana.[3]

Late in the afternoon we reached the road-junction at the foot of Jebel Heitan, where the Parker monument stands. Here we struck the Darb el Haj, the Moslem Pilgrim's Way, which in all probability is identical with the Biblical 'Way of Mount Seir' (Deut. i. 2). The road is covered to a depth of 4–8 inches in chalk dust which envelops the motorist in swirling clouds that penetrate every pore.

There is a good view of Jebel Heitan from the road-junction. It is a range of white, brown-topped peaks, with slopes of limestone deeply seamed by wind and rain. Its upright walls suggest those of a huge legendary palace adorned with innumerable white columns. At the foot of this marvel of natural architecture, about forty yards west of the roadside, is a gleaming white plinth surmounted by a monument which can be seen from far and wide.

We walked up the steps leading to the monument. It is a square stone-and-clay column about thirteen feet high. On two sides of the column are large marble

[1] Bar-Daroma, *The Negeb* (Heb.), Jerusalem, 1935.

[2] Incidentally, this range is a further candidate for the title of Mountain of God. See H. Wiegand, *Sinai* (1920), p. 54.

[3] M Jean Perrot describes these tools as 'typologically Upper Palaeolithic but chronologically of a later period'.

plaques bearing the inscription in Arabic and English: 'In Memory of EL LEWA
. . . Pasha, Governor of Sinai 1906–1912, 1918–1923'. The name 'Parker' has
been completely erased with some sharp instrument. Someone, prompted perhaps
by feelings of *pietas*, had written in the deleted name in black pencil on the monument: Parker.

The view towards Jebel Heitan, from the top of the hill on which the monument
stands, is extraordinary, resembling some lunar landscape; a dazzling whiteness, a
complete absence of vegetation or any other sign of life, the surface everywhere
jagged and cratered. The road from here forks west to the Mitla Pass, which
unfortunately I did not succeed in visiting on this occasion, and east to Qal'at el
Nakhl-Themed-Eilat.

It was now getting towards dusk. I knew that an army unit to which I had been
attached in the Israeli War of Independence was stationed hereabouts. They
would gladly put us up for the night. Someone in Bir el Hasana had told us that
their camp lay north of the road, not far from the crossing. We scanned the map
to see if we could pin-point the camp. In any case, a hasty glance at the map in the
fading light told us that north of the road lay a mountain with innumerable gullies,
any one of which would afford shelter for the night even if we failed to locate the
army unit. This mountain, Ruweiset el Akheider, rises to 2,620 feet, and is the
southernmost peak of a chain extending about twenty-five miles north to the
vicinity of the Nitzana–Ismailia road. According to the map there was also a
complete system of wells on the western side of this mountain range, but we had
gathered that this region was out of bounds to us for security reasons.

We reached the slopes of Ruweiset el Akheider in complete darkness. The moon
was not yet out. Hence, when the wheels of our car came up against a low wall,
which in the pale light of our headlamps seemed to us to be simply debris brought
down by the floods, we merely drove round it. Perhaps our extreme fatigue after
a day of driving in the dust was to blame for our paying no particular attention to
'these stones'. And then, when we found ourselves in a military camp—of the
unit we had been seeking—we forgot them completely. We were given a quick
meal and were soon asleep in one of the camp tents.

I was awakened in the middle of the night by the moonlight streaming in to
the foot of my bed through the open tent flaps. For the moment I did not know
where I was. It was so bright that I had no difficulty in reading by the light of the
moon the small print in which the wadis were marked on the map. I got up. All
was still. I walked slowly up the hill-side. The sentry indicated that he had recognized
me and let me pass. Soon I reached the top of a low hill at the foot of the main
peak and looked south onto the plain scarred with innumerable wadis reaching to
the huge Wadi el Bruq.

In these exalted surroundings I suddenly noticed the low wall we had bumped
into before, and now, in the bright moonlight, I recognized it as an old friend:
it bore a striking resemblance to the MB I stone dwellings of the Negeb and
Kadesh-barnea. I could hardly trust the evidence of my own eyes: the slope was
covered with ancient ruins. Could it be possible, that here, in the heart of this arid   Plates 22, 23
desert, a settlement from the beginning of the Patriarchal period once existed? In
a mood of mingled excitement and scepticism—it was pointless to look by moonlight for sherds which might confirm my tentative identification of the walls—I
returned to my tent. I tried to get to sleep but it was long before I eventually
succeeded.

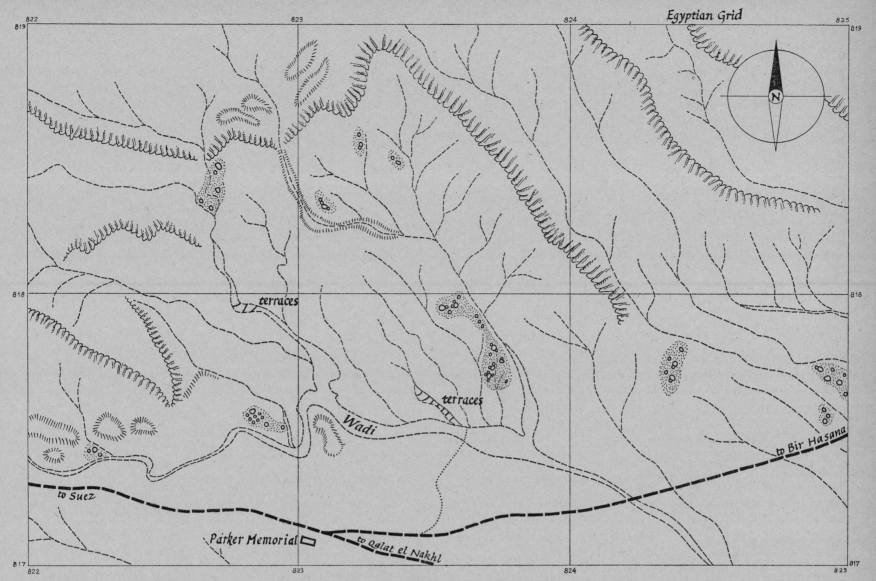

Fig. 8. Plan of the Canaanite remains on the slopes of the mountain Ruweiset el Akheider

At first light I sprung out of bed and roused my companions. Judge of my astonishment to see that half of the tent was itself in the middle of a large circle of stones, and that there were sherds literally at my feet. They were without a shadow of a doubt not only MB I, but indistinguishable from those found near Ain el Qudeirat. We checked on the map: the grid reference (Egyptian) was 823.4–818.5.[1]

We spent the whole day intensively searching on the slopes of Ruweiset el Akheider for ancient ruins and sherds. In the evening we tried to identify the site. The only Biblical reference that seemed to shed light on the problem was: 'And when we departed from Horeb, we went through all that great and terrible wilderness, which ye saw by the way of the mountain of the Amorites . . . and we came to Kadesh-barnea. (Deut. i. 19). 'The mountain of the Amorites' might well refer to our settlement, which to judge from its remains must have been inhabited for a considerable time. And Abraham and the battle of the kings . . . was the location of that story in this part of Sinai too? According to the Bible, the Amorites, Abraham's confederates (Gen. xiv. 13) dwelt with the Amalekites and other tribes, scattered throughout the desert from the Negeb to Sinai. Was this the mountain of the Amorites, one of their main centres? Perhaps also the 'Way of Shur' followed this route: Kadesh-barnea (El Muweilah) Bir-el-Hasana—Ruweiset-el-Akheider—

[1] In a short report, 'Messrs. E. H. Palmer and C. F. T. Crake in the Desert of the Exodus' published in *Our Work in Palestine* by the Palestine Exploration Fund in 1873,

Wadi-el-Haj—the Suez region. All these have adequate supplies of water.

But to return to the discoveries made during the day. Early on we found remains consisting of groups of two to three structures on a small slope above one of the wadis running east, at the southern end of Ruweiset el Akheider. As we climbed up the slope an imposing view of a large Canaanite settlement presented itself to our gaze. At first we estimated the settlement to cover an area of some five acres, but subsequently abandoned the attempt at delimitation, as we found Canaanite remains and numerous sherds as far away as a mile-and-a-quarter east of the wadi in which the first discoveries had been made. In the middle of this large settlement was a particularly large structure, which we measured.

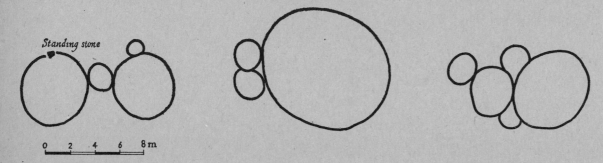

Fig. 9. Middle Bronze I dwellings

The remains of the settlement sprawl over a number of slopes in the area, and even in the gullies between the hills. They conform to a more or less uniform pattern: a large circle, sometimes several yards in diameter with a number of smaller circles adjoining. Inside the circles are hearths, near which is a heap of ashes covered with sand or loess. Add the most striking feature—a large upright monolith—and you have the typical MB I settlement from the Negeb to Ruweiset el Akheider. All these uniform remains are accompanied by an amazingly homogeneous sequence of sherds.

Later in the day we found a large tomb near the Pilgrim's Way, which runs at the foot of Reweiset el Akheider. It is a well-built construction of undressed stone, like all buildings of the period. Next to it was an exceptionally large circle nearly 11 yards in diameter. At this spot, where the ground was absolutely level, with no signs of flood debris, we dug inside the wall of the circle to a depth of about sixteen inches and found some sherds and a few flint implements. To our great disappointment time did not permit us to excavate the large tomb. However, we explored all the deep, bare gullies running into Wadi el Bruq, finding ruins over a wide area. Our impression was that there had been a settlement here of considerable size, numbering scores of buildings and lasting several generations.

Next morning we decided to avail ourselves of a commando car, the use of which we had been offered for twenty-four hours, to visit the oil city of Ras el Sudr.

After about ten miles of crossing numerous feeders of the great Wadi el Bruq we passed the wide path of Darb el Khutlieya. This road, which runs parallel to the Darb el Haj, meets another important desert road, the Darb el Shawi—it too runs parallel to the Pilgrims' Way from the Red Sea coast—at a point about six miles east of the road we had been driving alone. From this crossing a track runs south of the Pilgrims' Way, into the Wadi a-Raha and continues to Suez without touching

there is an account (p. 284) of several sites at the foot of Jebel el Ejmeh, south of Badiet el Tih, on which these scholars found a number of highly interesting early remains. Unfortunately I was unaware of the existence of these relics when I made my various journeys to Sinai and as far as I am aware none of the scholars who worked in Sinai during the Israeli occupation has attempted to investigate them. It may be of interest, therefore, to quote a section of this report which describes ruins similar to Canaanite and those which we ourselves found on Et Tih:

'Before ascending Jebel el Ejmeh the travellers [sc. Palmer and Drake] paid a visit to a place visited by Mr. Palmer the preceding year. It is called Erweis el Ebeirig, and is a piece of elevated ground covered with small enclosures of stone, not like those previously described. On the summit of a small hill on the right is an erection of rough stones, surmounted by a conspicuous white block of pyramidal shape. The remains of enclosures existed for miles round; the small stones which then, as now, served for hearth stones exhibited the action of fire. On digging beneath the surface charcoal was found in abundance, and outside the camp were a number of stone heaps which could be nothing but graves. The site, moreover, is a most commanding one, and admirably suited for the assemblage of a large concourse of people.'

As is his wont, Palmer endeavours to identify this site with a Biblical locality, in this case Kibroth-hattaavah. Since from here to Ain Hudherah is 'exactly a day's journey', he considers the latter site to be the Biblical Hazeroth (Num. xi. 34, 35). Although in the absence of reliable archaeological evidence it is not possible to accept Palmer's identifications, the existence of numerous ancient sites between the plateau of Et Tih and the mountains of southern Sinai is a fact of considerable importance. These sites are a continuation, perhaps, of the chain of MB I 'settlements' extending through Bir el Hasana to Ruweiset el Akheider and thence south through a pass between Jebel el Ejmeh and Erweis el Ebeirig and thence south to . . . Horeb?

the difficult Mitla pass. We paused for a moment to gaze on the Darb el Khutlieya; it was not often one came across a road that stood out in such clear relief against its desert background. It bore unmistakable signs of having been a major pathway for the passage of the caravans of antiquity. Its white stone surface had been worn so smooth by the feet of the camels, asses and men who had plodded along it in ancient times that it positively glittered. Much to our regret we could not spare the time to drive along this road and examine it more closely.

While we were waiting at the roadside one of my companions drew our attention to a flat-topped mountain standing apart in splendid isolation from its neighbours in the mountain range to the south of us. A glance at the map showed us that this was Ras el Gindi (2,142 feet). Even at the considerable distance it stood from us, it exerted a powerful impression, seeming to stand guard over the mighty plain that lay below it.

After about three miles we reached the declivity of Wadi Sudr. We drew up, amazed by the sight which confronted us. Before us lay a gleaming white wadi whose steep sides were completely bare, as if they had been combed by some enormous rake. The landscape resembled that of Jebel Heitan, but it was on an infinitely grander scale. Wadi Sudr itself is very similar to the great Wadi Jerafi in the southern Negeb, though the latter is not so white and its banks are less seamed.

Plate 28   Wadi Sudr extends for the whole of its length along the foot of Jebel Raha. Ras el Gindi itself is an advanced outpost of Jebel Raha, though the word 'Jebel' is misleading, as it is actually a plateau about 25 miles long by 18 miles wide, reaching a height of 2,602 feet at the summit. From here the road makes its way over the bed of the wadi or parallel to it. The surface of the road that wound its way into the wadi-bed had been churned up by the tyres of the innumerable vehicles that had preceded us recently. Ras el Gindi came closer into view. The great towered walls surrounding the summit of the mountain were now clearly visible.

It is difficult to convey the impression made by Ras el Gindi on the spectator who sees it from close up. In shape it resembles a cone sliced off the top and here stands a mighty fortress. Its foothills are composed chiefly of soft white chalk

Plate 29   which the wind and the rain have carved into pillars ascending vertically from the wadi to the foot of the middle slopes, so that the mountain appears to be based on columns of white marble. Straddling the top is a low, steep ridge of grey chalk. Undoubtedly this is the most beautiful and picturesque of Sinai's northern mountains.

It was not possible to climb up to the fortress, as we had promised to return the commando car by first light next day, and we still had some distance to go. From time to time we looked behind us and could see the fortress topping the mountain even from a distance.

We took the broad track east of Ras el Gindi, but it soon became clear that the ancient road, guarded by the fortress, ran along the other, west, side of the mountain, linking up with the Darb el Khutlieya continuing to Wadi Raha for Suez, and the El Nakhl road (Darb el Haj) or the Darb el Shawi for the Gulf of Aqaba.

After driving about two-and-a-half miles we could see a clump of date-palms in the distance, in Wadi Sudr. A glance at the map showed us that we were not far from the spring of Hesed el Milh and Ain Sudr. We drove on a little farther to find the entrance to the wadi, and turned into a clear track which brought us straight to the spring. We had come to an oasis; a group of palms tucked away in a tributary of Wadi Sudr, near a low, long hill. The effect of this precious oasis set down in the heart of yellowish-white limestone interspersed only occasionally with patches of dry, dusty green was indescribable. The soil was moist, the air keen and pure, and around us were the table mountains. We could hardly believe that this delectable vision of palm and green vegetation was not a mirage.

Plate 28

We followed the brook and came to the spring itself, which flowed from the white rocky bed of the wadi to form a small pool, less than a foot deep and only a few square yards in extent. The wadi near the spring is narrow and quite flat, formed from solid rock in which the pool seems to have been inserted. Shallow channels leading to the group of date-palms, about 150 yards from the spring, had been dug into the rocky wadi-bed, and the Beduin had dug a few irrigation channels by the side of which clumps of rushes were growing. The spring water was fairly salty and here and there the ground was covered with thin patches of salt. There was a rim of white salt even round the irrigation channels. A number of shacks on the hillside near the cluster of palms, remnants of camp-fires and camel-dung, attested that the spring had attracted a not inconsiderable number of Beduin. We searched for early remains near the spring, of course, but found nothing save some confused heaps of masonry, perhaps tombs, and no sherds.

We piled into the car again and drove down the wadi. The going was hard, the road frequently taking hairpin bends. As it was late and we wanted to reach the 'oil city' while it was still light, we did not stop even when tempted to do so by ruins near the road which we should have liked to investigate. At one place, which I was unable to identify with certainty—it was near Bir Abu Garad—the road took a sharp turn into a small valley well protected by the steep banks of the wadi. As we entered the valley, which resembled in shape a huge reservoir, we passed a number of defensive positions evidently built by Beduin for whom the valley must have served as a permanent, well-guarded camping-site. Many characteristic Beduin structures were still to be seen in the valley, but I am of the opinion that it would amply repay thorough archaeological investigation. It may well be that early remains would be found. At the exit of the valley, too, on each side of the road, we found defence-posts built of stone, clinging like birds' nests to the rock. On the wall at one of these posts we could see a drawing of ibex and camels; the work, no doubt, of a Beduin who sought relief in art from the tedium of guarding the entrance to the valley.

We reached the western tip of Jebel Raha. To our left rose a lofty mountain with three sharp pinnacles. The mountains of Et Tih cannot be said to convey any aura of Sinaitic grandeur, but the traveller who sees the three peaks of Jebel Somar rising gracefully but powerfully to the sky from deep, criss-crossing wadis becomes aware that he is approaching the granite mountains of southern Sinai.

Our prospects of reaching the oil city while it was still light now seemed remote. A last steep pass brought us out onto the stretch of desert, about thirteen miles wide, leading to the seashore. We were driving fast, and only occasionally could we make out a tomb—a heap of stones by the roadside—or scanty relics of some temporary encampment.

Suddenly, as if by split-second scene-shifting, the dark-coloured range of the Egyptian mountains and the thin gleaming line of the Gulf of Suez came into view. We drew up to the outskirts of Ras el Sudr in a final burst of speed, and after a mile or two found ourselves on a well-made, asphalt road that soon brought us into the oil city.

A long line of buildings, well laid out in a semi-circle on the wide sandy shore of the Gulf of Suez, provided the oil field's dwelling accommodation. Derricks lined the roadside, pipelines led in all directions, huge containers glinted into the clear sky. We passed some weird constructions of steel, looking like Christmas trees; the first signs of a great scheme of desert oil development.

Urbanity was provided at a cross-roads by a sign reading 'Fifth Avenue'. We drove towards the beach. On both sides of the road we saw large pools of black liquid, presumably crude oil that had leaked from the pipelines, staining the gleaming sand.

Night fell rapidly. The sunset over the African granite mountains proved a memorable experience. The looming shadows of the mountains on the darkened horizon contrasted vividly with the blood-red rays of the setting sun. The sky, flecked with tufts of small white clouds, changed from pale to vivid red, to pink, to pinkish-white, and finally to white against a sable background.

The first part of the drive back was uneventful, though we had some difficulty in getting out of the network of roads in the 'oil city'. Every time we did a right or left turn we found ourselves back where we started. However, eventually we took a curve which brought us into the wadi along which we had driven into the city in the fading light of the evening. How different the scene looked now, in the light of an enormous moon dramatically silhouetting the mountains. Only our driver, who found it difficult to see the road in the blinding moonlight, was unimpressed. When we came to the first gradient we saw the silvery sheen of the Gulf of Suez and the African mountains overlooking it. The white limestone all around us gleamed in the moonlight. We estimated that four to five hours' driving would bring us to Parker's Monument, where we would bivouac. The whiteness all around seemed to drive the cold into our marrows.

Two hours' driving brought us to the entrance of Wadi Sudr. The wonderful rock of Ras el Gindi looked down on us, and in the moonlight I could see clearly the great wall that crowned its summit.

It was then that the idea came to me. I stopped the car. My companions awoke and looked at me questioningly. 'Let's climb to the top,' I said. There were about ten of us all told—a number of hitch-hikers had attached themselves to us at Ras el Sudr. Everybody except the driver, who was obviously worn out, thought it was a splendid idea.

We drove the car off the road as near to the rock as we could and started the 500-foot climb on foot. Ras el Gindi is very steep; on the south side it is sheer cliff, so that this route was out of the question. We decided, therefore, to tackle the ascent from the north side. Even this was stiff enough. Sheer steepness is no obstacle if there is something firm to hold on to. But crumbling chalk, on which every step sets a small avalanche in motion, is nerve-racking. We scrambled up the lower foothills without difficulty, but very soon found ourselves with such a narrow foothold that eventually we were walking almost on a razor's edge. Right and left loomed the dark abyss. In the last stages we moved very quickly—a nervous haste. As we came close up to the wall our difficulties ceased, to our grateful surprise. We were even able to find a track that had been preserved in places, and in thirty minutes we had reached the fortress.

The climb had warmed us, but we were now exposed to a strong wind and intense cold. We looked for a way in to the fortress, and in the north-west corner of the wall we found an enormous gate that might have been made for us. To make us feel at home, the builders of the fortress had carved a large Shield of David in the middle of a great arch which welcomed us. A mass of large well-cut blocks of stone lay nearby. Over the gate we could see the flourishes of an inscription written in beautiful arabesque letters. The gateway was built in medieval Arab style, the stone-cutting being of a remarkable precision. The arch was composed of at least thirty blocks of stone, all fitting together so finely that a hair would not go between them. We passed through the gate and found ourselves inside a fortress made up of a number of large buildings. The surrounding wall, in perfect preservation, gleamed in the moonlight. We walked its whole length. What had appeared from below to be bulges in the wall were now seen to be the towers of the fortress, complete with loopholes. The wall was shored up in parts with huge perfectly preserved wooden beams. At the end of the wall, where the hill bulged a little, an enormous round tower, also with loopholes, had been built.

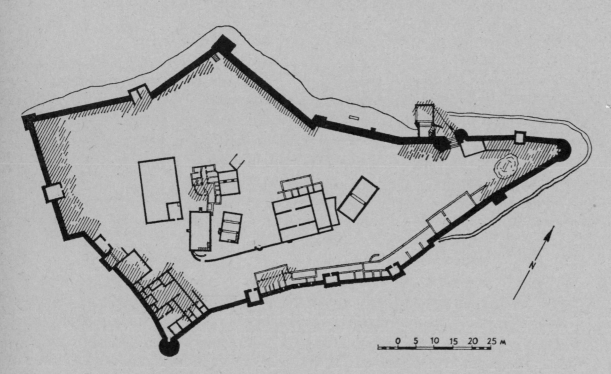

Fig. 10. Qal'at el Gindi (J. Barthoux, Syria III)

Powerful as was the aesthetic impression produced on me by the fortress, it also aroused my archaeological interest—I had not been aware of its existence. I began looking for sherds in an attempt to date the masonry. I clung to the hope that I should be able to find some early sherds amongst those collected in the dark, but was disappointed when I inspected the pottery at daybreak. The fortress of El Gindi was built (by Saladin) at the end of the twelfth century.

Among the other 'sights' of this wonderful fortress we found a fine arch with a delicately incised drawing of two ibex and a lintel decorated with a remarkable geometrical drawing crowned by a representation of a dove with outstretched wings. We also found an enormous roofed cistern, many yards deep, lined with smooth blocks of stone shaped to form a huge soaring vault. In the heart of the complex of buildings stood a large mosque. Nearby were great underground water cisterns.

Just before midnight we had reluctantly to start back. We reached our rendez-vous at 3 a.m. and were able to snatch a little sleep before setting off again into the wilderness of Et Tih. The great monotonous stretch of gravel plain and the myriads of gullies intersecting the road every few yards made the trip a penance.

After two hours driving we reached the village at Qal'at el Nakhl, and stopped

Plate 26

to examine the fortress which had been built by the Turkish Sultan Selim I in the course of his conquest of Egypt in 1517.[1] It was used as a hospice by Moslem pilgrims. It is a square machicolated building, with round towers at the corners, typically Arab in style and splendidly built when one takes into account the remoteness of the site. Here and there the building has been restored. Over the gate are

Plate 25

three inscriptions dating from different periods.

Numerous chambers were built onto the fortress walls. On the north side of the courtyard stood a large ruined, roofless building, which seemed to be a very recent addition. Between this building and a smaller one (also ruined—perhaps only partially built) adjoining it, grew a huge zizyphus. In another corner of the courtyard a second gate aroused my curiosity. It guarded the entrance, I found, to a mosque which, though it had apparently never boasted a permanent roof, housed

Plate 24

a *mihrab* of the most delicate workmanship in the southern wall.

We had found much to excite our imagination on our journey along the Pilgrim's Way: the soft limestone rock gleaming in the sunlight from the polish imparted by the tread of a multitude of camels and pilgrims alike; the fortress of El Nakhl with its most interesting mosque and the two huge reservoirs nearby. These testified to the great efforts made by the Sultans to ease the rigours of the pilgrimage, to protect the pilgrims from the hazards of man and nature, and, above all, to gain control of the Peninsula.

East of the fortress is a sheikh's tomb, and around it are hundreds of Arab graves. The large cemetery is clearly of some antiquity, but prolonged searching failed to uncover any early sherds. This, and the appearance of the buildings in El Nakhl and environs, suggest that the site is not pre-medieval.[2]

[1] At the beginning of the nineteenth century, Mohamed Ali, after thoroughly repairing the fortress, constructed the modern buildings in the courtyard and made some additions to the mosque.

[2] L. Eckenstein, *A History of Sinai*, 1921, p. 2. 'It was known in the middle ages as a *puteus Soldani* (well of the Sultan).'

Apart from its 'sights' El Nakhl had little to commend it. We found its squalor and general air of desolation depressing, and were not sorry to leave. In any case, our time had run out, and so we had to take the short way home (we should have liked to return to Israel via Eilat and the Arabah). Once more we found ourselves driving between barbed wire and pill-boxes till we came to the great wadi-bed; the broad, smooth, barren plain of Wadi el Arish. Then we struck north.

'AND WHEN we departed from Horeb, we went through all that great and terrible wilderness' (Deut. i. 19).   ET TIH

The plateau occupying the centre and the northern part of Sinai—about two-thirds of the whole Peninsula—is associated in Beduin tradition with the wanderings of foreign tribes in the remote past; hence its name: the desert of the '*Tih*' ('Wanderings'). The foreign tribes were the Israelites, their wanderings those of the Exodus.

South from a line Eilat-Suez, the plateau rises imperceptibly to culminate in Jebel el Tih and Jebel el Egma (the latter reaching a height of 5,250 feet). Here at its southern extremity it ends abruptly in steep crags.

Wadi el Arish has its source in this high plateau, and when the rains come its waters tumble along thousands of watercourses to pour themselves into the mighty 'River of Egypt'.

In the Bible we read of two roads cutting across the plateau: the way of Shur and the way of Mount Seir. These roads are still in use. The first is the Nitzana (El Auja)—Ismailia road, and second is the 'Pilgrim's Way' (Darb el Haj) from Eilat to Suez. In Biblical times the few existing water sources in the 'great desert' determined—and to a great extent determine even today—the course followed by these roads.

Hour after hour the traveller journeys over vast gravel plains enclosed on all sides by mountain ridges. Hour after hour the view remains unchanged: deep blue skies above, a plain of limestone and gravel below; and surrounding the plain, the mountain ranges seemingly cut to a uniform height by some gigantic razor. Occasionally there is a surprise: a well with a fine ancient khan close by; a spring of water, and near it a huge mountain fortress and unexpected ruins dating from the days of the Patriarchs.

At twilight the great wilderness assumes an aspect of surpassing beauty. There is a constant change of colours: pink, brown, purple; and with the lengthening shadows a constant change of scene. Time stands still.

HAMADA 21

The most characteristic feature of Et Tih (the 'Wilderness of the Wanderers') and the southern Negeb is the bare unending gravel plain (*hamada*), with never a glimpse of water or vegetation. It comes as a surprise to find that anyone ever lived there and yet numerous flint implements of various Ages have been discovered: Middle and Upper Paleolithic, as well as Mesolithic and Neolithic implements.

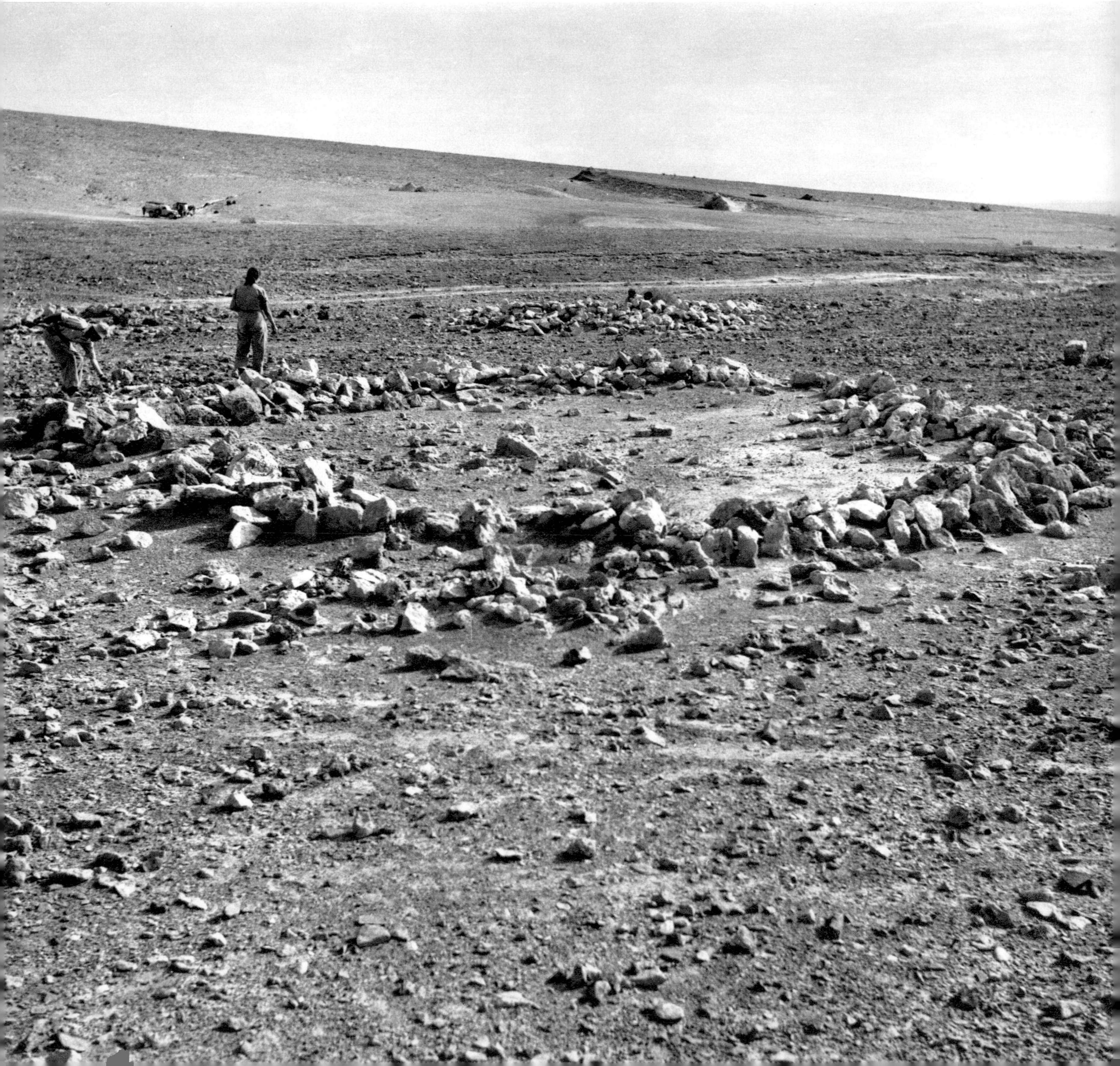

24

25

22 REMAINS OF HOUSE AND COURTYARD, EARLY PATRIARCHAL PERIOD, IN CENTRAL SINAI

The greater part of the buildings discovered on the slopes of Ruweiset el Akheider belonged to dwellings of the pattern usual in the Negeb and Sinai in Middle Bronze Age I: a small house with a circular courtyard attached. The remains that were discovered here show that the dwellings were in use for a prolonged period.

23 REMAINS DATING FROM THE EARLY PATRIARCHAL PERIOD, FOUND NEAR THE MITLA PASS

Extensive remains of buildings dating from Middle Bronze Age I, i.e., the beginning of the Patriarchal period, have been discovered north of the road-junction of Sudr el Haitan, on the slopes of Ruweiset el Akheider, and not far from the memorial to the former Governor of Sinai, Colonel A. C. ('El Lewa') Parker. This discovery was a cause of some surprise, as the region had previously been considered completely barren wilderness. The sherds gathered near the ruins are similar to contemporary sherds in the Negeb and other parts of Israel. We must assume, therefore, that the wave of Amorite migration extended to the centre of Sinai, at least.

24 MIHRAB IN THE MOSQUE OF THE FORTRESS OF EL NAKHL

In the grounds of the fortress stands a large building in several stages of construction, but added after the fortress itself was built. This is the mosque of the fortress. In the south wall of the mosque are two mihrabs, one above the other. The upper mihrab is shown in the picture. It is about 13 feet above ground-level.

The mihrab indicates the direction in which the worshipper in the mosque has to pray. In origin it is simply that part of a palace where the ruler sat on his throne, or the niche containing the statue of a Christian saint. There are grounds for believing that the use of the mihrab was taken over by Islam from Christianity. The mihrab of Qal'at el Nakhl surprises by the excellence of its masonry and its beauty of form—it was probably brought here pre-fabricated from distant parts.

25, 26 FORTRESS OF EL NAKHL

Qal'at el Nakhl was once one of the chief townships on the Pilgrim's Way. It is situated almost midway between Eilat and Suez. Qal'at el Nakhl—'Fortress of the Date-palms'—was built by Sultan Selim I at the beginning of the 16th century. There are three inscriptions over the entrance to the castle, differing in date and character. The first records repairs to the fortress carried out by Sultan Ahmed III in 1705; the middle one dates from the end of the 18th century, and the third is the earliest in date of all. (Communicated by Mr A. Ben Chorin, of the Hebrew University.)

LIMESTONE MOUNTAINS AND FLINTY GRAVEL 27
PLAIN IN WADI EL HASANA

This is the most desolate-looking region in the whole wilderness of Et Tih. The eye sees nothing but the black gravel plain bordered by flat-top limestone hills of a blinding whiteness. Wadi el Hasana flows round Jebel el Halal on the south-west and is swallowed up in the desert sands north of Bir el Hasana.

AIN SUDR AND RAS EL GINDI 28

Ain Sudr is a small spring at the lower end of Wadi Sudr. The spring's water is salty, but drinkable. Nearby is a small grove of date-palms and numerous bushes. On the horizon, about two miles north of the spring, can be seen Ras el Gindi.

SALADIN'S FORTRESS ON RAS EL GINDI 29

Three roads traverse the desert of central Sinai: that of Wadi el Arish, that of Wadi Sudr or El Raha, and the Darb el Haj or Pilgrim's Way. Ras el Gindi stands at the junction of these three routes, the only ones practicable for caravans. This explains the importance of the great fortress erected by Saladin at the end of the 12th century on the summit of a mountain (2,142 feet) that stands isolated from the other peaks of the region, as an outpost of Jebel Raha. The fortress played a decisive role in Saladin's campaigns.

PART FOUR   THE ROAD TO THE ISLE

In Wadi Umm Sideira and Jeziret Fara'un

The end of February 1957 found us *en route* for Sinai again. This time we decided to make Eilat our base, from which we would explore the seaport's western and southern approaches—Ras el Nagb and environs, and the isle of Fara'un in the Gulf of Eilat-Aqaba. We also thought we would try to reach the 'Valley of the Inscriptions' in the hills south-west of Eilat. We had read in the newspapers that new rock-inscriptions had been discovered in this valley by members of a geological survey group and included a fine drawing of a typical Jewish candelabrum (Menorah) and a ram's horn (Shofar).

We set out from Ras el Nagb, on that stretch of the Darb el Haj ('Pilgrim's Way') which runs direct from Sinai to the shore of the Gulf of Eilat, passes through Tel el-Kheleifeh and continues east to Aqaba. We had used the ascent of Ras el Nagb on more than one occasion, on visits to the beautiful spring of Ain Netifim and on archaeological expeditions in the mountains of Eilat up to the frontier. This time the way was open for exploration beyond the boundary. We set out to traverse the country which till now we had been able only to gaze on from the Israeli border: the jagged peaks near Wadi Umm Sideira and, of course, the wadi itself, with its interesting inscriptions.

The road from Eilat to the police post of Ras el Nagb had been built for the pilgrim traffic as far back as the reign of the Fatimite Caliph Ahmed Ibn Tulun (868–84), and subsequently it would appear to have been rebuilt by the Mameluke Sultan Nasser Ahmed Ibn Qalun (1293–94).[1]

We learnt from a stone inscription discovered as Ras el Nagb that the last Mameluke Sultans too (at the end of the 15th century) saw to it that the track, vital for the pilgrim traffic to Mecca, was kept in good repair. In this inscription the last of the Mameluke Sultans, El Ashraf Khansuh el Ghuri, is mentioned as having ordered 'the cutting of this blessed road'. This formula led Jarvis to conclude, wrongly, that the road was originally built by Khansuh el Ghuri. Jarvis states that the stone had been re-erected by the Frontiers Administration and set in a bed of concrete at the head of the pass—we decided we would look out for it as soon as we reached the police building at this spot. The road was also repaired in 1831 by Ibrahim Pasha to enable him to transport his artillery down it for the conquest of the Hejaz.

I was disappointed not to be able to find any reference to the Biblical 'Way of Mount Seir', for this route traditionally followed the Darb el Haj very closely.[2]

[1] J. Brasslavi, *Know your Israel* (*Ha-yadata et Ha-aretz*) (Heb.) (3rd ed., Tel-Aviv, 1956) Vol. 3, 'To Eilat and the Red Sea', pp. 461, 467, 469; Dr Z. Vilnai, *Transjordan, the Hauran and Sinai* (Heb.) (1946), p. 247; Jarvis, *Yesterday and To-day in Sinai*, I, 1931, p. 126.

[2] See fig. 4.

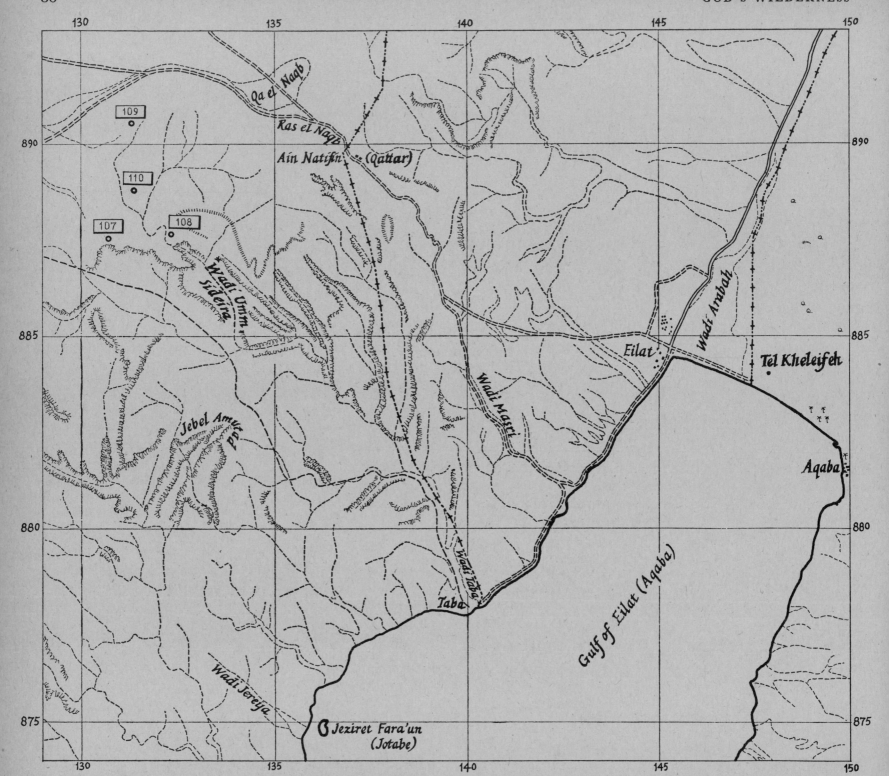

Fig. 11. The Gulf of Eilat (Aqaba) and the mountains of Eilat

On the Peutinger Map, too, a road is marked from Eilat to Egypt.[1] We hoped to find traces of this Roman road, and perhaps pre-Roman remains, on the important Ras el Nagb–Eilat sector of the Darb el Haj route. I myself was particularly anxious to see if I could find any early remains in these parts like the early Patriarchal (MB I) remains our party had found at the intersection of the Darb el Haj and the Bir el Hasana–Kadesh-barnea road (though not at El Nakhl) and I had high hopes of finding Canaanite relics either here or near the road leading to the Sinai plateau.

We entered the Eilat mountain region by the Nahal Shlomo (Wadi Masri). Though I had driven up and down this beautiful wadi several times before at all hours of the day, the rugged landscape of grey-reddish peaks and gravel-and-sand wadi-beds still held me in thrall. By day the rock-face of the mountains is harsh and cruel, but in the twilight hours, in the dark crimson glow of the mountain-tops and with the rays of the setting sun casting hard shadows among the peaks, it is supremely beautiful.

On this occasion we drove along the wadi early in the morning. We stopped only once on our way to the frontier post of Ain Netifim, on the great bridge, when we tried to find some inscription or ruins or anything else that would tell us who the bridge's builders were. We were unsuccessful in our search, but could see that the bridge had originally been much lower, about six feet above ground. Subsequently a new span had been built over the old, raising the bridge to about twelve feet above the level of the wadi. At this spot the road surface is good, being laid on a specially-built foundation.

We now drove our wheezing Land-Rover cautiously round hairpin bends, and suddenly found ourselves looking down on a magnificent view: beneath us was a ravine some 600 feet deep—the road had climbed steeply from Wadi Masri (about 1,300 feet) to the summit of Jebel el Kireikal (about 1,950 feet)—separating us from a cluster of dark granite peaks of extraordinary beauty. Behind them we could glimpse the dark-blue waters of the Red Sea and still further in the background the high wall of the dark-red mountains of Edom. When the sun shines on this scene, as it did when we reached the top of the road, the Red Sea seems a silver tray gleaming against a background of almost black granite mountains hemming it in.

At Ain Netifim we reached the frontier again. The road now took us through a plain fringed with hills and then, after driving on fine golden sand, we reached the Egyptian post of Ras el Nagb with its police-station. We passed many heaps of stones, *rujum*, some of which were burial cairns and others connected with Beduin superstitions. We looked very closely for sherds, but found none earlier than the Mameluke period. We searched near the ruins of primitive structures, presumably old Arab dwellings, but the only sherds we found were medieval. The sherds and masonry we found on the slopes of the hill crowned by the Egyptian police post were all Arab, too.

It was evident to us at this initial stage that the present road (part of the great Darb el Haj) from the plateau of Et Tih to Eilat winding down from Ras el Nagb through the steep pass of Eilat, was very largely an Arab road that had been built to serve the pilgrim traffic. At all events, in spite of intensive search we failed to find anything earlier than the Arab period. In the course of our subsequent explorations we ascertained that the more ancient road went south of Ras el Nagb straight down the mountain-side to Taba. I shall revert to this later.

[1] The Tabula Peutingeriana shows the principal lines of communication and the distances between the various road stations of the Roman Empire in the year 170 A.D. It was discovered in the Library of Vienna in 1753.

The police post at Ras el Nagb, which we had so ardently desired to see at close quarters in the past, also proved disappointing. The building itself is fairly new. It is in the form of a large courtyard built of stone and clay and has several large rooms. It would seem that a flat-roofed concrete structure with gun slits in the walls had recently been added to the courtyard. We toured the building hoping to find, perhaps, some old masonry that had been re-used, and also the stone tablet inscribed with the name of Khansuh el Ghuri. We found no old masonry in the walls of the courtyard, but fixed to the northern wall we did find a monolith about a foot-and-a-half high embedded in concrete. It was intact and well preserved and contained four lines of ornate Arabic script. We photographed the stone confidently thinking it was the Khansuh el Ghuri monument.

Plate 86

(A few months later I called on the late Mr Uri Ben Chorin, the well-known Arabist, in the library of the Department of Archaeology of the Hebrew University at Jerusalem, to ask for his help in connexion with literature on the Darb el Haj and other places in Sinai. Mr Ben Chorin willingly examined a number of Arabic inscriptions which I had photographed in Sinai; at El Nakhl, at Qal'at el Gindi, Wadi Umm Sideira and elsewhere. It did not occur to me to ask him to examine the Ras el Nagb inscription, as I felt sure it had been published, but I presented him with the photograph, thinking he would like to have a new 'snap' of the tablet. He took the photograph, looked at it, and pronounced: 'This is not it!' I was surprised, but when Mr Ben Chorin read out the inscription to me I realized he was right. It transpired that instead of the el Ghuri tablet—which could not be found in Ras el Nagb—we had found and photographed an inscription the existence of which had previously been unknown. We had made a new Sinai discovery—in the archaeological library of the Hebrew University. The inscription we had photographed states in so many words: 'In the name of Allah the compassionate and the merciful this building was repaired in the name of the mighty, victorious Sultan Hasan and the mighty and victorious Sultan Mohammed Qul'aun on the 7th Rajab in the year 747 (=27th October 1346).' And so we have a new date to add to the list of dates on which the road (for it is probable that 'this building' must include the road itself) was repaired, and a new name to add to the names of those who catered for the comforts of the pilgrims on their arduous journey to the Hejaz.)

It is interesting to note that neither Robinson nor Bartlett mentions the existence of any building at Ras el Nagb at the time (1838–56). Presumably the present police post was erected much later, probably in the present century.

After resting for a short time at Ras el Nagb, we drove on and came to the plain of Qa el Nagb. To our surprise the ground was covered, over the area of an ellipse about a mile-and-a-quarter in length, with smooth, firm, yellowish-white marl. There were indications that an airfield had been constructed on the plain. Here and there we saw groups of stones arranged in circles, but no sherds or other archaeological indications. Probably the stones were for keeping down tents.

Plate 70

The groups of dark-coloured isolated stones projecting from the great gleaming plain, the black hills encircling it, made a remarkable sight, the like of which I had never witnessed before. To add to the weirdness of the spectacle, we witnessed a mirage: a blue lake fringed with date-palms in the shade of which nestled a small brilliantly white house. The picture was quite clear, the lake quite close.

We reached the canyon of Wadi Umm Sideira late in the afternoon. It was obvious that in the few hours before dark we should be unable to inspect and photograph all the finds that had been made in the wadi, still less explore the surrounding area. We decided, therefore, to come here the next two days as well. An account follows of the extensive exploration we undertook of the district during these two days, and of the ancient sites we found.

After leaving the Darb el Haj, which at this spot consists simply of numerous parallel tracks, we found ourselves in pathless territory. We followed a tyre track which we hoped would lead us to the canyon. The going was now difficult, occasionally over sandy wadi-beds, branches of the Wadi Umm Sideira, which we were hardly able to negotiate. Again we were driving over *hamada*; this time the plain was covered with shingle. It was an utterly bleak and desolate region, without soil or water for man or beast, displaying the ravages of the climate: hot by day and bitterly cold at night, with winds of gale force and rare but torrential rains. The jagged mountains descended precipitously to the Red Sea.

I stopped the car near a pile of gleaming stones that had stood out in the distance against the dark *hamada*. It was an ancient burial tumulus the stones of which, at some time or other, had become dispersed. We found a number of similar tumuli nearby, as well as some sherds, Nabataean-Roman, but could establish no connexion between the sherds and the tumuli. We also collected a considerable quantity of flint implements here, including two Neolithic scrapers. (This site is marked 109 on Fig. 11).

We drove on southwards. After about a mile-and-a-quarter we stopped near some heaps of rough, undressed stones, laid out in large clear circles on a hill-side gently sloping down to a small wadi that twisted its way southwards (Site 110). They seemed to be of great antiquity, and in their vicinity we collected many fine flint implements: scrapers, gouges and notched blades, all Upper Palaeolithic. I climbed on to the summit of the adjacent hill to get a good photograph, showing topographical features of the site. It made a fine picture of a 'station' tucked away in its wadi-bed; a little hidden from view, and sheltered from the winds by the hill.

Plate 21

Leaving the wadi, we climbed on to a plateau of *hamada*—gravel strewn with black flint—where we found more ancient burial mounds and flint implements. One spot remained indelibly engraved on our minds on account of the superb view it commanded (Site 107). It lay on the very edge of the plateau, not far from a good road running south into the wadi-bed some 650–950 feet below us. Here, too, we found numerous graves, and flint implements of the same Palaeolithic type we had found previously. Again we were unable to establish any link between graves and implements. From this site we had a magnificent view of the chain of peaks and hills scored by gullies and canyons of coloured Nubian sandstone. The sun now stood low in the western sky, and the lengthening shadows filled the wadis with delicate tints of blue. The hill-tops glowed crimson against the backdrop of the Red Sea. On ridge and ravine, on jagged rock and deep-cut wadi-bed lay an infinite peace. It was only after we had drunk our fill of the scene that we noticed a path on our left which descended precipitously into the wadi-bed deep down below and passed south-west of Wadi Umm Sideira in the direction of Wadi El Howara.[1] It had evidently been extensively used. Here and there we found well-constructed passes. Evidently in ancient times this was a main route to Taba (the track links up, in fact, with those of the Darb el Haj and Darb el Gaza).

We drove east to a small intersection of wadis on which stood two tumbledown Beduin huts. This was the landmark the late Dan Gilead, the original discoverer of the inscriptions in Wadi Umm Sideira, had given us as a guide to the entrance to the canyon. Although there were obvious signs that Beduin encamped here-

[1] When we reached Wadi Umm Sideira and found there was no way out to the south we walked for about five miles along this path till we came to the peaks of Wadi Haneish. From there we could see clearly the road to Taba. As there was no pass from here back into the canyon of the inscriptions we had to go round the group of hills to reach Wadi Umm Sideira and our car again.

abouts, we were unable to find even a patch of soil suitable for cultivation, nor
could we discern any wells or water-cisterns. It may be, however, that among the
innumerable intersecting wadis, there were water-sources which we failed to notice.

Before describing the wonderful canyon of the inscriptions itself it may be as well
to give a brief account of the entrance to the wadi and of the adjacent hill-sides.

On the slopes surrounding the wadi, which at this spot forms a small valley,
we found many ancient ruins, sherds and flint implements. This was the site of a
great, well-established, Nabataean-Roman-Byzantine camping ground, the largest
we had seen in the whole region. The soft and clean soil of the valley, and its
sheltered position made it eminently suitable for encampment.

From the top of the hill one gets a good view of this traditional camping site,
which drew travellers from far and near. One can see the great natural water-holes   Plate 73
nearby, the canyon with its important inscriptions, and it needs but little imagination to see the whole animated scene as it must have existed in the past.

The ruins consisted of crude circles formed of small boulders and of large
pebbles; the typical indication, together with the relevant sherds, of a temporary
camping site in the Negeb or Sinai. Most of the sherds we collected were Roman-
Byzantine, but some were clearly Nabataean-Hellenistic. Here, too, the flint
implements included some of Palaeolithic type, such as we had found elsewhere
in this region.

We went down into the deep wadi-bed, which widens out before the entrance
to the canyon itself. The ground consisted of gravel and sand, and everywhere
there lay huge pieces of rock that had fallen from the cliff above. Here also a surprise
awaited us: on a sandstone boulder jutting out from the ground—one of many
scattered in profusion throughout the wadi-bed—we saw numerous small cup-   Plate 80
marks with quite deeply-incised grooves among them. A few crude drawings of
ibex or similar animals had also been scratched on the boulder, near the cup-marks.
The strange sight provoked one of my companions to conjecture that the boulder
was a primitive altar. But what was an altar doing here? Had it fallen from the
hill-top, or been swept along by floods from elsewhere? The boulder was about
6 feet long by 4 feet wide. We could not ascertain its height, as it was deeply
embedded in the ground. For a long time we stood round it discussing its possible
significance. Perhaps because of an inner resistence to any explanation of a religious
or cult origin, I hazarded the surmise that the cup-marks and incisions indicated a
whetstone, used for sharpening the implements with which the inscriptions in the
canyon had been executed. However, it was easy to counter every suggestion with
another, and the prolonged discussion failed to yield any firm conclusion.

At the end of the small valley formed by the wadi-bed is a narrow, eight-foot-wide
ingress to the canyon, the walls of which range in height from 25 to 65 feet. Just
above this ingress, to the right, is a fine Greek inscription, as if to welcome the   Plates 71, 83
traveller seeking the shade of the canyon.

Inside the canyon all was still. The spectacle defied description. The grey-pink-
yellow-white cliff-like walls contrasted with the blue of the vaulting sky above.
Wind and water had scored innumerable deep fissures and indentations in the
rock-face. Everywhere the effects of water wearing away the soft sandstone could
be seen. The torrents that had poured into the canyon from above had left their
clear imprint all along the walls.

Immediately on entering the canyon we were greeted by inscriptions and rock-
drawings: long Nabataean inscriptions and short Greek inscriptions, and many

Plates 74, 76, 79

drawings of horned beasts—ibex, probably. These rock-drawings were like old friends to me, for I had come across them in their thousands in the mountains of the Negeb, mostly Nabataean-Roman-Byzantine, as were the majority of the drawings here.

Plate 78

Nearly all the inscriptions in the wadi are on the east wall of the canyon, where it slopes inward in concave fashion, thus being protected from the ravages of the spate coming from above, and affords a broad flat surface of smooth rock for writing on. The west wall, on the other hand, is distinguished by its numerous drawings of ibex, whole herds of them along the length of the wadi. After some twistings and turnings the narrow canyon opened out into a square—about 25 to 30 feet wide—and with a thrill of excitement we found ourselves in a great 'hall' crowded with inscriptions. Taking pride of place in the centre was a large drawing,

Plates 77, 85

executed with some skill, of a seven-branched tripodal candelabrum, with next to it a ram's horn and another, indeterminate object. Above the candelabrum was a Greek inscription, clear enough for us to read—AKRABOS—and to the left an inscription in Latin—VICTORIA AUGC—presumably commemorating Augustus

Plates 81, 82, 84

Caesar. About ten feet above the ground was a lintel-like projection, some fifty feet in length, covered with row upon row of fine, clear Nabataean inscriptions. Superimposed on these were also a few Greek inscriptions, obviously of later date. Most were in groups of three short lines.

Plate 75

As I stood in front of the drawing of the candelabrum to photograph it I suddenly saw a second drawing of a candelabrum, resembling the first, on the opposite wall. It would seem that both had been drawn by the same 'artist', but the second had been engraved on a part of the wall washed by flood water coming from above, and its outlines were less clear. There was no other drawing near it; neither inscription nor Shofar.

As darkness began to fall we made our way towards the farther end of the canyon, about 150–200 yards from the 'Hall of the Inscriptions and Candelabra'. Here the canyon terminates in a waterfall—in flow only in times of spate—which

Plate 72

descends to a depth of about 220 feet, the soft sandstone, with its pastel colouring, being carved out into fantastic whorls. We had not been the first to thrill to this astonishing spectacle, for on the west wall, immediately above the waterfall, we found a number of Greek inscriptions and drawings of camels engraved on the rock-face. On this west wall there is a smooth surface, about 7 feet high and 30 feet long, covered with drawings and inscriptions. Most of the drawings were of horned beasts. There were also a number of Arabic texts of antiquity on this wall, some of them again superimposed on earlier drawings.

The great waterfall spanned the whole width of the canyon, making it impossible for us to get out. Incidentally, it had not been at all easy for us to get from the 'Hall of the Inscriptions' to the waterfall. In many places floods had made deep hollows in the wadi-bed, and it was only by clinging to the ledges and hopping from one foothold to another that we had been able to reach the waterfall at all. There could be no question of any road ever having passed through the canyon. This being so, we asked ourselves why it had been singled out for so many inscriptions and drawings. Had this extraordinarily beautiful canyon been chosen as a camp-site offering welcome shade to travellers along the not-far-distant road, as well as water (for an appreciable part of the year the hollows in the ground would have been filled with water)? To me this seemed an inadequate explanation; I had seen many camping-grounds in Sinai, full of Nabataean and Greek rock inscriptions, but always alongside a road. One great ancient route had the inscriptions on the cliffs overhanging the road itself. The conclusion seemed inescapable to me that the canyon had been a sanctuary, a traditional place of prayer or worship for travellers in Sinai camping nearby—not in the canyon itself, which is highly unsuited to camping. Before the last lap of their journey to the Red Sea or before setting out on the hard trek through the wilderness of Et Tih they would gather here in thanksgiving. Even to-day the square in the canyon could serve as a military field-chapel. Perhaps this might offer a clue to the 'altar' at the entrance to the canyon.

The two Jewish candelabra (Menorot) in the canyon—of their Jewishness there can be no question—are of particular interest. They are quite exceptional among the Sinaitic inscriptions that abound throughout the south of the Peninsula. We tried to guess their significance. Had they been drawn by Jewish merchants who had come here to pray, and thought to 'consecrate' the canyon with their drawings? Among the many inscriptions in the canyon, were some written by Jews?

Plates 75, 85

Plate 84

The canyon of the inscriptions in Wadi Umm Sideira is one of the most beautiful and interesting of the places we visited in our explorations of Sinai. It is a matter for regret that we were unable to investigate the whole area thoroughly.[1]

We returned to our base, Eilat. Our second objective was Jeziret Fara'un, the beautiful islet about which we had heard so much. Before setting out I had read a number of books, new and old, to see what they had to say about the island and its history. I found to my surprise that hardly one of my authors had explored the island thoroughly. Some had merely written what others had copied from others; only occasionally had an author actually paid the island a fleeting visit. The picture in my mind after reading these various authors was confused, to say the least. What intrigued me greatly was to read that there were remains 'dating from the Exodus' on the island as well as modern buildings built by the Beduin.

Plate 40

I quote a frew brief extracts from some of these books, beginning with a description by Dr Robinson, the famous Sinai explorer and scholar:

'At ten o'clock we were opposite the little island, which we judged to be a good quarter of a mile distant from the shore. It is merely a narrow granite rock some three hundred yards in length, stretching from northwest to southeast with two points or hillocks, one higher than the other, connected by a lower isthmus. On it are the ruins of an Arabian fortress with a battlemented wall running around the whole, having two gateways with pointed arches. This is without doubt the former citadel of Ailah, mentioned by Abulfeda as lying in the sea. In A.D. 1182 it was unsuccessfully besieged with ships, by the impetuous Rainald of Chatillon; and in Abulfeda's time (about A.D. 1300) it was already abandoned, and the governor transferred to the castle on the shore. The ruins therefore cannot well be referred to a period later than the twelfth century.'[2]

Currelly, a co-worker of Flinders Petrie's, thus describes the island after he had visited it:

'Near the bend of the Gulf of Aqaba there is a tiny island called Jeziret Fara'un, on which there is a Turkish castle of early date. . . . The walls of the castle show very poor workmanship, many of them being mere rubble; and all are thin, and must have been of very little protection against any weapons heavier than arrows. The cisterns, however, are well made, with very flat vaults that appear to be still perfectly solid.'[3]

Woolley and Lawrence (1914–15) examined the island more thoroughly than their

[1] The expedition of the Department of Antiquities led by Mr Moshe Dothan spent only a few hours in the wadi and was able to see and transcribe only a limited number of transcriptions. Probably owing to fading light they failed to notice the second candelabrum-drawing. Unfortunately the results of Mr Dothan's expedition have not yet been published.

[2] E. Robinson, *Biblical Researches in Palestine*, etc., Vol. 1, 1841, pp. 237-238.

[3] C. T. Currelly, in W. M. Flinders Petrie, *Researches in Sinai* (1906), pp. 264, 265.

predecessors. I want to quote some extracts from *The Wilderness of Zin* that will help the reader to follow the description of the island which I give later myself:

'The Crusaders called it [the island] Graye consistently. It is, as seen from the shore, a small double island formed of two sharp points of rock, about 50 feet high each, united by a strip of sandbank raised only a few feet above the level of the sea. . . . This island has been strongly fortified at various periods. All round the shore at sea level are to be seen the remains of a wall built of rough masonry about 4 feet thick, entirely destroyed down to the level of the beach. The Aqaba water seems to have a curious effect of petrification (perhaps due to the coral there), which cements the shores into a single slab of conglomerate; this wall therefore looks as natural a tipped stratum as need be, save for the tool-marks still showing in the inner edges of some stones. The date of this first wall it is impossible to determine.

On the sandbank which unites the two peaks lie half-buried some rough stone huts and circles, and there is also on it a little pool of salt water, perhaps 50 yards long. It is now filled with sand and débris, but has been deeper, and probably had an entrance from the sea. Set around the pond, as though for ornament, are some drums of columns in soft white limestone. There were two similar drums in a keep of the northern building, and (from their stone-dressing) they seem of different period from the rest of the place. Of course they may well have been shipped across from some ruin at Aqaba.

The pottery found in it [the castle on the island] was, however, not very early; practically all of it was metallic-glazed. The pottery of the north end of the fort was nearly modern, and its abandonment may have been as recent as a century ago.'[1]

Fig 12

Woolley and Lawrence mention the plan—rather poor and not particularly accurate—of the island made by Léon de Laborde, and P. Savignac's study published in 1913. This was in fact the only attempt at an accurate, scholarly investigation of the island to have been published down to the present day.[2]

Nelson Glueck paid a hurried visit to the island in 1926. He was able to collect some sherds, and his report on them is the first scholarly assessment of the island's pottery, and as such of importance in determining the island's identity. After a brief discussion of the buildings on the island, Glueck writes:

'Despite a careful search, the earliest sherds found were *Byzantine*,[3] while the predominating sherds were medieval Arabic. We found nothing that could be said to be definitely Crusader, and the writer is inclined to share Savignac's belief that the present ruins represent buildings erected by the Saracens.'[4]

Finally, a quotation from an expert on Sinai, Miss L. Eckenstein, who was at one time Flinders Petrie's assistant in his Sinai explorations:

'Saladdin, in 1170, had a fleet built, with which he sailed around the peninsula, and attacked and retook Aila. But the enterprising Renaud de Châtillon (the Alairis of Makrizi) collected material for ships on the Dead Sea, conveyed them to the Gulf of Akaba on camel-back, and seized Aila from where he pillaged the coast, and made piratical descents on the shipping for over a year. The small island Iotabe, later Emrag, the present Jeziret el Faraun, lies at a short distance from Aila. It has no harbour, but is almost entirely built over by a castle with squared towers in the medieval style. The work was probably begun in Roman times, but was added to by Renaud de Châtillon. But in 1184 Melek el Adel (Abu Bakr, 1199–1218), the brother of Saladdin, came with a fleet to Aila and attacked and finally routed the Franks.'[5]

[1] Woolley and Lawrence, *The Wilderness of Zin*, pp. 145, 146.

[2] R. P. Savignac, '*Une visite à l'île de Graye*' in *Revue Biblique* (1913), p. 588. See also A. Hashimshoni's study in this volume, with new map, fig. 16.

[3] My italics.

[4] Nelson Glueck, *Exploration in Eastern Palestine, III*, AASOR (1939), p. 11.

[5] L. Eckenstein, *A History of Sinai* (1921), p. 148.

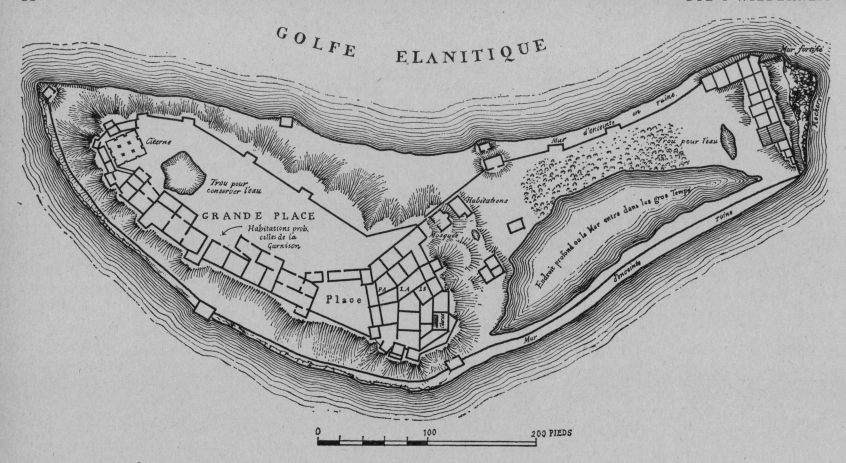

Fig. 12. Map of Île de Graye (Jeziret Fara'un), redrawn from that by Léon de Laborde

What is interesting for us in the foregoing extract is that the authoress takes it for granted that Iotabe and the island of Fara'un are one and the same. It is a matter for regret that Miss Eckenstein deviated in this instance from her usual practice of citing her authorities.

Jotabe, incidentally, was in the past usually identified with the island of Tiran in the south of the Gulf of Aqaba, but the Hebrew University expedition to Tiran was unable to find any archaeological evidence for the equation of the two places.[1]

The begetter of the equation was Procopius, who lived in the sixth century A.D. He describes a voyage in the Gulf of Aqaba, and the island of Jotabe, which he says lay a thousand stadia from Aila. He says that once past the island there was nothing but the broad sea ahead. To the right of the Gulf the coast had disappeared from view, so that it was necessary to keep to the left in order to be able to anchor each night. Sailing at night was dangerous because of tempests and also because of the numerous shallows in the Gulf. A thousand stadia are roughly 120 miles, a mile or so more than the distance of Tiran from Eilat, and as there was no other island in the Gulf that tallied so well with Procopius's account, his identification was accepted without question.

According to Procopius there was an autonomous Jewish settlement on the island which was brought to an end about 535 A.D. during the reign of Justinian. The Jewish historian Graetz describes this settlement as a 'Jewish kingdom' which, he avers, 'withstood the Persians, Greeks and Romans, and did not vanish from the pages of history until the reign of Justinian, Emperor of Byzantium.' The tenacity of the island's Jewish population, as asserted by Graetz, seems to rest on

[1] See Dr Aharani's discussion of this, pp. 161 ff of this volume.

the fact that a Persian, Ammorcessus, who governed the island in the reign of Leo, expelled the Byzantine customs officials from it and thus secured control of the commerce in the Gulf and the Red Sea. The Israeli historian, M. Avi-Yonah, writes:

'In all probability, a Jewish colony established itself on the island during the governorship of Ammorcessus. They also settled in the town of Maqna, some 25 miles to the north of Tiran, on the Red Sea coast. The Emperor Leo acknowledged the rule of Ammorcessus in 474. The Romans under Anastasius, reconquered the island in 498 A.D., but, no doubt for financial reasons, did not molest the Jewish settlers, who continued to be an autonomous community until the reign of Justinian.'[1]

According to Avi-Yonah, a Jewish colony established itself on the island under Ammorcessus. Who, then, lived there before that? I sought an answer to this question on my return from Jeziret Fara'un, and found it, I think, in an article in Pauly-Wissowa's Encyclopedia. The article refers to a *History of the Emperor Leo*, by the fifth-century Malchus of Philadelphia, in which it is stated that the Jews, who till then had controlled, from the island, the shipping in the Gulf of Aila,[2] were expelled from the island by Ammorcessus.[3] If this is so, and bearing in mind also that the island was conquered by the Romans (from the Jews?) in 429 A.D., then the Jews could have returned to Jotabe only towards the end of the 5th century A.D., when the island had been conquered, according to Theophanus, by a Roman general after prolonged fighting against the Arab successors of Ammorcessus. The general farmed out the collection of dues from merchant vessels reaching Aila to 'Roman merchants' who were experienced in this kind of activity, viz., the Jews who had previously lived on the island and been expelled by Ammorcessus. When this 'autonomy of the Jewish community in Jotabe' came to an end under Justinian the island was settled by Christians. We read (in Alt, the famous German historian) of a 'Bishop of Jotabe' taking part in an episcopal synod.

No wonder, then, that Israeli scholars were keenly interested in Jotabe and, identifying it with the island of Tiran, were anxious to see if they could discover any relics of the 'autonomous Jewish community' there.

Our own group, however, had no thoughts of Jotabe when we left early in the morning of 23 February 1957 for Taba. Yet the result of our exploration during the next few days was the identification of Jotabe with Fara'un.

Our plan was to see Taba and then to drive down the coast till we reached a point opposite Fara'un. We did not expect to be able to visit the island itself, and wished only to see it and photograph it from the shore. We knew that there was a romantic fortress on the island, Crusader, Saracen or early Turkish, with later additions.

It was very pleasant, driving along the shore of the gulf in the mild light of the early morning. A quarter-of-an-hour or so after leaving Nahal Shlomo (Wadi Masri) we saw, in the distance, the picturesque clump of Sudanese date-palms sheltering the well of Taba. These palms differ from those normally found in Sinai in that they have a number of branches ascending more or less vertically and are crowned with a fan-like foliage. A similar group—the only other one we know of in this area, is to be found near Ain Defiyeh (Ebrona) north of Eilat.

Taba itself was deserted. We found nothing of any interest near the well, and although we knew that a search of Wadi Taba for early remains would have been in all probability rewarding, we pressed on towards the island, leaving two long

[1] M. Avi-Yonah, *In the days of Rome and Byzantium* (Heb.) (1946), p. 173.

[2] According to A. N. Pollack, *History of the Arabs* (Heb.) (1945), pp. 58 ff., the Aila of antiquity was built on an island near the northern shore of the Gulf of Eilat (Aqaba). It mustered a population of some three hundred souls and could only have been the present *Jeziret Fara'un.* Unfortunately the author cites no authorities to support this statement, but in view of the archaeological finds on Fara'un it certainly merits serious consideration.

Plate 48

[3] Pauly: *Realencylopädie d. Classischen Altertumswissenschaft*, ed. G. Wissowa, *s.v.* 'Jotabe.'

deep tyre-marks in the sand behind us. At the back of my mind was the hope that we might after all be able to visit the island, and in any case I was afraid that later on the sun would be right overhead and I should be unable to photograph it even from a distance. And now it came into view: a twin-domed rock rising from the dark-blue sea. The walls of the island's fortress sharply silhouetted in the sun, the mainland mountains ranging in colour from grey to red overhanging the island: all combined to take a powerful hold on the imagination.

We climbed a hill south of the island strait. Here we sat awhile and took some photographs. From here we could clearly make out the two hills of the island, with the fortress on top, and between the hills a kind of shallow lake. Apart from ourselves, not a soul was in sight. There was a gentle ripple on the sea. The mountains of Edom on the horizon were veiled in a deep-blue haze. The harbour of Eilat lay hidden somewhere behind the mountains.

Plate 40

We looked at the map. Behind us the narrow, steep-banked Wadi Qureiyeh widened out a little to reach the shore. The name Qureiyeh recalled to us the Crusaders' name for the island: Le Graye. Dr Robinson had noticed that both names were variants of the same word, meaning 'a village'.[1] We found ourselves wondering whether, after all, there might not be a surprise awaiting us on the island; could it be that among the walls of the fortress we might find traces of a *Qirya*, of a small, ancient settlement?

The same evening we were sitting in the 'Tnuva' canteen in Eilat, a little depressed because we had failed to secure a dhow to get us to the island, when the door opened and a group of visitors entered. One of my companions recognized a student friend among them, who told us that a group of Haifa Technion students under Avia Hashimshoni, senior lecturer in architecture, had arrived at Eilat in the afternoon. They were going over to the island the next day to make scale drawings of the ruins. There and then we changed our plans and decided to join the Technion group.

We did the run along the western coast of the Gulf in a large motor-launch. After the students had landed on the island near the tower F3, we did a complete trip round the island to enable me to photograph it from all angles from the sea.[2] Thus I was able to obtain a complete panorama, as it were, of the island, with its walls, ramparts, rocks, citadel and towers. Even on this preliminary photographic reconnaissance I could see that the remains on the island were numerous and complex, and that we should have to think very carefully how to spend our limited time on the island if we were to study them properly. Two courses were open to us: we could join the students in their comprehensive architectural study of the island, or we could photograph it in minute detail for subsequent interpretation.

As soon as I stepped on to the island and noted various archaeological features I saw that it would be of great interest and importance to make a thorough survey of it. I spent a few hours, therefore, walking round the island, taking the opportunity to look for sherds by which to date the various kinds of masonry I had seen. At the outset I had noticed that there were various stages of fortifications: some early, on the narrow strip of shore, some later, and some perhaps even modern.

[1] Dr E. Robinson, *Biblical Researches*, Vol. I (1841), p. 237.

[2] In describing sites and masonry on the island I shall refer from now on to the new map of the island drawn by Avia Hashimshoni, p. 186.

I started my exploration of the island from the northern end. Here there is a strip of shore about 16 yards wide between the sea and the rock surmounted by a very solid fortress wall. I had already formed the impression, at this spot, that the strip and the fortress on the northern hill belonged to different parts of history. This impression was confirmed when I discovered very clear traces of a casemate wall

Plate 43

all along the area of the shore, partly submerged in the shallow water of the sea and partly on the shore itself. I was struck by the curious way in which the rough unhewn stones, strengthened with loam or some similar cement, were bonded. They covered the shore to a width of about seven feet. I walked all along this wall and noticed that every 7 to 10 feet a clear line of stones crossed it transversely, dividing it into more or less equal sectors. This puzzled me until I realized that all this masonry was in fact the foundation-remains of a solid casemate wall, and the lateral lines of stones were simply the inner walls forming the casemates (Plate 43, in which, in the lower half of the picture, a lateral line of stones can clearly be seen 'cutting across' the wall). The stones had been specially bonded to provide the strength necessary for the wall to resist the beating of the waves and to stop the water from seeping into the chambers from underneath. I walked round the whole island, and everywhere I saw the foundation-remains of the casemate wall, its chambers and towers. At the eastern side of the island could be seen the foundation-remains of at least three massive square towers built of exceptionally large and heavy blocks of unhewn stone. The remains of tower F6 were particularly clear. About 6–7 feet inside this tower I found a heap of sand and rubble which seemed to have been used as a filling for a wall the large stones of whose 'skin' had disappeared.

My view, which I hold as firmly now as I did then, was that the heaps of material dotted about the island, about 3–6 feet in from the shore-line, were remains of a wall later than the casemate wall which was subsequently demolished, perhaps so that its blocks of stone could be used to build the wall and citadel on top of the hill. The matter was decided when I later reached the great tower F3, still preserved to a height of 16–20 feet. This tower is made up of an early foundation stratum consisting of very rough undressed stone rising to a height of about 5 feet and linked at sea-level with the foundations of a casemate wall part of whose length is submerged. On these foundations smaller, partially dressed blocks of stone were laid. The upper part of this tower joined the later wall built about 6 feet in from the shore-line, as may still clearly be seen.

Walking south from the tower at F6 I encountered another puzzle. Within the broad area marked H between hills A and B I found some parallel lines of masonry bonded in the same way as that of the wall surrounding the island. Avia Hashimshoni thought the walls were part of buildings of a small settlement that once existed here, the narrow streets of which ran parallel to the outer wall of the island.[1]

We succeeded in finding a quantity of sherds on the island, many of which were medieval Arabic. Others were later than this, while among the ruins of the citadel, particularly at the northern end of the island, were some which were quite recent. We found very few sherds along the shore-line, mostly Roman-Byzantine. Only in the area of H did we find early sherds. Some of these sherds were very crude, painted in red-brown on almost white slip. We have not been able definitely to identify these sherds as yet, but I should not be surprised if they turned out to be Iron Age I. As no comparative material is at present available, the question remains undecided.[2] We tried to 'scrape' the soil, but the ground was very hard and without proper digging tools it was impossible to get down to any depth.

From the area H we walked to the other side of the island. Here too we found masonry the construction of which indicated that it was much earlier than anything on top of the island's two hills. Around the 'pool', D, once stood solid stone buildings. The pool itself was a well-built inland harbour which in course of time became

Plates 43, 46

Plate 45

[1] Unfortunately I could only devote a day to the island, but Avia Hashimshoni spent a few days on it, in the course of which he made a thorough examination of the citadel and also inspected the wall surrounding the island. See his contribution to this volume, pp. 185-189.

[2] At the time this English edition goes to press, I concluded a thorough exploration of Wadi Arabah and its ancient copper industries. The pottery, investigated during this exploration, furnished enough comparative material for the definite identification of the sherds found on Jeziret Fara'un as Iron Age pottery of the 10th century B.C., the period of King Solomon. Details of this exploration and its implication for Biblical History will be given in my forthcoming book on the Wadi Arabah. See preliminary Reports: *Illustrated London News*, Sept. 3rd 1960, p. 383: "King Solomon's Mines, A new discovery"; *Bible et Terre Sainte*, 1960, pp. 4-10: "Les mines du roi Solomon."

silted up to such an extent that it now resembled nothing so much as a large puddle. Here we found a Byzantine capital. A second capital was found in the northern citadel. Skirting the harbour, we found ourselves following another man-made wall, E, separating the harbour from the sea. At one end of this wall, F1, were clear traces of a tower. Between this tower, and another square tower opposite, F2, ran the channel from the sea to the harbour.

I climbed to the top of hill A to get a general picture. It was clear enough: a casemate wall around the island, and between the two hills a small settlement with its harbour and warehouses. If we take into account the rooms of the casemate wall, too, it will be seen that the inhabitants of the island could dispose of ample storage facilities. It is a great pity that all the buildings—at H, the rooms of the casemate walls, the harbour warehouses— have completely disappeared. They were demolished intentionally and the stones used for other purposes.

The whole complex of masonry suggests a settlement much earlier than we had expected to find on the island, antedating the Crusaders and Saracens and most probably even pre-Byzantine. In any case, Jezirat Fara'un is the only island in the gulf of Eilat that has masonry and sherds dating to the Byzantine period and has, therefore, to be identified with Jotabe. This identification can be upheld even should early remains and pottery be found on the island.

One detail which struck me may be mentioned here. I found a large block of hewn stone, in a window of the northern fortress, in which a fine Cross had been incised. Immediately I jumped to the conclusion—it was a case of the wish being father to the thought—that this proved that the Crusaders had in fact built here. Fortunately, subsequent reading and discussion with knowledgeable friends saved me from persisting in this *gaffe*. The Cross *per se* could, of course, have been Byzantine; we know that a Christian Church existed on the island of Jotabe in Byzantine times. However, it is quite likely that the blocks of limestone were brought from the shore at Aqaba, perhaps even being taken from ruins on the mainland.

Plate 44

The evidence of settlement on Jeziret Fara'un lends fresh interest to the former Arabic name of the island and the nearby wadi on the mainland: *El Qureiyeh*, corrupted by the Crusaders to *Île de Graye*. Qureiyeh and the Hebrew Qirya, 'city', are cognate; additional evidence for the existence of an early Jewish community on Jeziret Fara'un, the beautiful island set in the Gulf of Eilat-Aqaba in the Red Sea.

AROUND SINAI'S
SOUTHERN COASTS

THE SOUTHERN COASTLINE of Sinai is a broad sandy strip into which large wadi-estuaries debouch, and along which are situated the traditional stations of the Israelites on their journey to the Mountain of God. Marah, Elim and the station 'by the Red Sea' (Num. xxxiii. 10) are indelibly stamped on the memory of the pious and still have the power to lure travellers of various faiths in pilgrimage. It is difficult to resist comparing the traditional descriptions of places and the stories told by travellers of a bygone age with the actual scenes that present themselves today on the route from Suez to Ras Mohammed and from Sherm el-Sheikh north to Eilat. 'Pharaoh's Bath', for example, proves disappointing: it is no more than a rather curious sulphurous spring on the coast. And Ain Marah is non-existent; the modern Ain Hawara, with which it is identified, is sanded up.

As night begins to fall the austere beauty and power of Jebel Serbal weave their spell. Tor, a small fishing village in the Gulf of Suez and a station for Christian pilgrims to Mount Sinai and for Moslem pilgrims to the Hejaz, takes on the quality of a fairy tale against such a background. And to traverse the plain of El Qaa is a moving experience. Sherm el-Sheikh, a small bay and a still smaller port, and Tiran, the island facing the new Egyptian fortifications on Ras Nusrani, are gems in a pale blue sea.

The Gulf of Eilat (Aqaba). Again a broad stretch of sand with the lofty mountains of Sinai looming in the distance. Here and there a few tall curving date-palms testify to the existence of groundwater and the digging of wells in days gone by. Dhahab, Taba and Jeziret Fara'un—names that will excite the interest of scholars and historians for many years to come—have now been explored for the first time and shown to be, respectively: the Biblical Dizahab and Jotbathah and the Byzantine Jotabe.

Our journey round the coast of Sinai ended in view of the mountains of Edom, at the port of Eilat, beside the Biblical Ezion-gaber, where King Solomon made a fleet of ships and where Israel has now established a busy, modern seaport.

30 THE TERRAIN, DETAIL

Sinai's broad southern littoral is for the most part a sandy waste. In the wadi-estuaries and in a few depressions between the sea and the mountains of Sinai the yellow sand is relieved by white patches of chalk and limestone, sometimes mingled with loess. In such parts there is water and vegetation: tamarisks, date-palms and acacias. But the parched soil shrivels and crumples up in the fierce desert heat.

HAMMAM FARA'UN—'PHARAOH'S BATH' 31

At the foot of the northern end of Jebel Hammam Fara'un gush forth hot springs—their temperature reaches 158°F.—which form the subject of a Beduin legend, according to which it was from Jebel Hammam Fara'un—'Pharaoh's Bath'—that Moses looked down upon the destruction of Pharaoh and his host, and it was here, too, that he indited his Song of Deliverance (see Ex. xv. 1). The water of these springs has an evil taste and smells strongly of sulphur. The two chief springs with a few smaller ones have their source about 12 yards from the shore, and flow into the sea. In the cave near the springs the temperature reaches 104°F.

THE GRANITE MOUNTAINS OF UMM BOGMA 32

Through steep canyons the path winds its way to the famous manganese mines of Umm Bogma. The manganese deposits are found in sandstone patches in the granite mountains. Umm Bogma is about 20 miles from Abu Zenima, where the British-owned Sinai Mining Company built a plant and small port.

AIN HAWARA, THE BIBLICAL MARAH 33

Pious pilgrims and Christian scholars have always striven to identify the Biblical stations of the Israelite tribes in their migration from Egypt to Canaan. The first of these stations after the parting of the waters of the Reed Sea was Marah. The Biblical Marah is nowadays identified with Ain Hawara, a spring now completely buried in sand. Only a cluster of date-palms and a damp spot nearby are there to tell of its existence.

THE BAY OF EL MARKHA, THE ANCIENT 34 EGYPTIAN PORT OF SOUTHERN SINAI

In 1948 Professor W. F. Albright found the remains of a small ancient Egyptian settlement (120 feet by 60 feet) near Bir el Markha, south of the modern mining port of Abu Zenima. It had served (15th-12th century, B.C.) as a transit camp for Egyptian miners on their way, by sea or land, along the Gulf of Suez to Serabit el Khadem. The bay of El Markha is a beauty spot which also attracts travellers who know nothing of the place's historical interest. Not far from the shore Dr Y. Aharoni found more remains. The chalk and limestone mountains overlooking the coastal depression are of dazzling whiteness.

WORMWOOD ON THE SANDY SOUTH-WESTERN COAST 35

Row upon row of wormwood plants line the desolate broad coastal belt of south-west Sinai and keep the soft sand from shifting. They give the impression of having been expressly planted for this purpose. The wormwood has small greenish-yellow flowers, and fragrant but bitter leaves.

33

34

35

36

38

39

44

45

36 TOR

This is the largest settlement in southern Sinai, boasting a population of about 1,000, mostly Moslems. There are about seventy Christians of Greek origin who constitute the 'middle class' of the town. They own fishing boats or are engaged in trade. Most of the inhabitants are fishermen or work in the quarantine station for Mecca pilgrims, which is well equipped with canteens, a hotel and a hospital. Tor has a monastery and Greek Orthodox church attached to St Catherine's. A few remains point to the existence of an ancient monastery, perhaps from the 4th century, and a Phoenician settlement has also been conjectured. In the photograph Jebel Serbal can be seen in the background dominating the port.

37 THE PLAIN OF EL QAA

This great *suaeda* stands on the plain of El Qaa, not far from the highway that runs down to Tor. The *suaeda* belongs to the beet family. It grows on salty soil such as is found near the coast. Its small, fleshy leaves store up water to sustain it in intense heat and drought and its flowers are yellowish-green.

38 THE STRAITS OF TIRAN

The island of Tiran is situated at the mouth of the Gulf of Eilat (Aqaba), 110 miles south of Eilat. Together with the smaller island of Sinafa it guards the entrance to the Gulf from the Red Sea. Coral reefs in the narrow straits render them dangerous to navigation. In the narrowest part the distance between Tiran and the Sinai peninsula is about 4 miles, and there is only a narrow channel between the reefs and both sides of the Straits.

39 SHERM EL SHEIKH

This bay is one of the beauty spots of the coast. A small tongue of land splits it into two: the south-west part is Sherm el Sheikh proper, while the eastern part is Sherm el Moiya. The varied colours of the surrounding mountains to the south and west, their upper parts black and their lower a dark red; the vast masses of coral to the north and the pale-blue waters of the bay lapping against a background of bright sandstone—all conspire to render the scene one of unusual enchantment. Although its bay affords anchorage, Sherm el Sheikh has never been inhabited until recent times, when it was used by the Egyptian forces as a small military port. In Sherm el Moiya there is a small sulphurous spring, but here too there was never a settled population—at all events no remains of any settlement have been discovered on the site.

JEZIRET FARA'UN IN THE GULF OF EILAT (AQABA) 40

This small island (350 yards long, 165 yards wide) at the head of the Gulf of Eilat (Aqaba) is known by various names. Beautiful corals off its shore led the Israelis of Eilat to call it the 'Coral Isle'; the Beduin call it 'El Qreiya', from which the name of 'Graye' which is was given by the Crusaders is derived. 'Qreiya', in turn, is probably a corruption of the Hebrew *Qirya*, 'city', recalling some Early Iron Age settlement on the island, or the Byzantine Jotabe.

Previous travellers and explorers considered Jeziret Fara'un to be a 'Crusader Fortress' and the site of battles between Crusaders and Saracens. Apart from the one fact on which everybody is agreed, namely, that the island was not fortified earlier than the Middle Ages, accounts of the island's history tend to be largely contradictory.

During Israel's occupation of Sinai a survey of the island was undertaken by Beno Rothenberg. This showed clearly that Fara'un was settled long before the Middle Ages, as the remains of the strong fortifications that were discovered testify. The sherds discovered prove that there was settlement on the island in the Early Iron Age and the Byzantine period. At all events, the finds made support the identification of the island with Jotabe, the Jewish settlement on an island in the Gulf of Eilat (Aqaba) that lasted to the 6th century A.D.

PALM HUT 41

At Ras Atantur, almost half-way between Sherm el Sheikh and Dhahab, there is a small oasis with a few huts built entirely of trunks and branches of palm trees. They are used by Beduin who come down from the mountains for the fruit harvest and fishing season and then abandon the oasis again for the mountains.

OASIS OF NABK 42

On the very shore of the Gulf of Aqaba, about 6 miles north of Ras Nusrani, the new Egyptian coastal stronghold, lies the oasis of Nabk. A broad flat plain runs parallel with the sea and the mountains, and on the edge of this sandy tract is a small group of tall date-palms, in the shade of which are a few rude huts, decaying and abandoned. Nearby is a well; it is difficult to say when it was dug.

THE CASEMATE WALL SURROUNDING JEZIRET FARA'UN 43

The illustration shows the remains of the eastern part of the strong wall that surrounded the island. The line of the inner wall is clearly visible, as well as the foundation of the party-walls that formed the casemates. A great part of the foundations of the outer wall lie below the water. In the centre the foundations of a square tower can be seen. See map, p. 186.

44 THE CROSS IN THE CASTLE WINDOW

This clearly cut Cross appears in the northern window of the fortress which to all appearances is of late (12th–16th centuries) Moslem construction. The Cross is incised on the surface of a block of clear white limestone, not locally quarried. There are a number of other limestone blocks in the upper part of the fortress. At first sight the Cross would appear to be linked with a Crusader fortress on the island, but further reflection shows that this is unlikely; firstly, because there are grounds for believing that the limestone, including the block of stone with the Cross, was brought here from ruined buildings on the shore of Aqaba, and secondly because the Cross may well not be a Crusading cross at all, but Byzantine (a Byzantine church is known to have existed on Jotabe). Nevertheless, the late Mr A. Ben Chorin considered that the masonry of the limestone—as shown in the photograph—places it definitely in the Middle Ages.

45 TOWER WITH ANCIENT FOUNDATIONS

At the west of the island is a tower the square foundations of which are built of large unhewn blocks of the island's granite. These foundations antedate the Islamic fortifications on the island's two hill-tops. They are part of the ancient casemate wall that surrounded the island.

46 ANCIENT TOWER BY THE SEA

On the eastern shore of Jeziret Fara'un the foundations of a square tower connected with the wall round the island can be clearly seen. These foundations are built of huge blocks of roughly-hewn stone, obtained from the quarry in the southern part of the island. The coast of Saudi Arabia facing the island can be clearly seen in the photograph.

47 LATE ADDITIONS TO AN EARLY FORTRESS

On the hill-top at the northern edge of the island of Fara'un lies the most recent addition to the Moslem-Crusader fortress shown in Plates 40 and 45. The masonry of the wall is reminiscent of the Turkish wall of Jerusalem. Remains of living-quarters occupied by the last people to inhabit the island—Egyptian troops and fishermen—are discernible in this part of the fortress.

48 TABA

The Egyptian frontier post of Taba lies about 6 miles south of Eilat, and about half a mile on the Egyptian side of the boundary. Near the estuary of Wadi Taba there is a deep, and probably early, well, and nearby a clump of fine Sudanese date-palms. The Nubian sandstone and dark granite background delight the eye. Near Bir Taba, and particularly in Wadi Tuweiba a mile or two to the south, Professor B. Mazar's team discovered ruins of many ancient buildings, some from the Roman-Byzantine period and some perhaps still earlier.

Dr Y. Aharoni identifies Taba with the biblical Jotbathah, one of the stations on the Exodus route.

KADESH-BARNEA AND
MOUNT SINAI

YOHANAN AHARONI

PART FIVE   KADESH-BARNEA AND MOUNT SINAI

I

COMPARED with the territory of Israel, though not with the deserts of Arabia, the Sinai peninsula assumes extensive proportions. Within it are vast plains of gravel, known to the geologist as *hamada*, endless expanses of undulating sand-dunes, great coast depressions, and high jutting mountains. By far the greater part of the territory is practically barren, such vegetation as there is being of the typically desert kind, meagre and monotonous. But there are exhilarating oases with tall, graceful date-palms, too. Most of the oases are small, and have little water, but some stretch for miles, with plentifully bubbling springs. They are situated both in the coastal plains near the shore and in the deep wadis between the towering rocks.

The historical importance of the Sinai peninsula lies in two factors: the geographical—Sinai's position between Egypt and Palestine and the Arab countries and the economic—the natural resources of its mountains.

As a land bridge between Egypt to the west and Palestine and the lands of the Fertile Crescent to the east Sinai was always a centre of international communications. In the north three important roads, named in the Bible, crossed the Peninsula.

Fig. 1   The most northerly was the famous *via maris*, 'the way of the land of the Philistines' (Ex. xiii. 17) leading from Egypt along the coast to the Philistine settlement of the Palestine littoral. South of this was the 'Way to Shur' (Gen. xvi. 7) leading from the region of Kadesh-barnea to a point, roughly the site of the present Ismailia, in the centre of the land strip from which the Suez canal was dug. Here were strung out the Egyptian fortifications known as *Shur Mitzraim*, or the '*Wall of Egypt*'; hence the names 'Way to Shur' and 'Wilderness of Shur' (Gen. xvi. 7; Ex. xv. 22). The coastal road was used primarily by the Egyptian armies and was bordered by a chain of water-holes, khans and strongpoints. The road south of this, on the other hand, was used by travellers from the Negeb to Egypt, who when they reached the fortifications of Shur were subject to Egyptian frontier control. The southernmost of the three roads led from the head of the Gulf of Suez to Eilat. To-day known as the Darb el Haj or the Pilgrim's Way, from its use by pilgrims to the Hejaz, it probably corresponds to the Biblical 'Way of Mount Seir' (Deut. i. 2), as the road continued from Eilat straight to the mountains of Edom, or Seir as they were formerly called.

To the south of the 'Way of Mount Seir' is the Sinai peninsula proper, bounded by the Gulf of Suez on the west, the Gulf of Eilat (Aqaba) on the east, and sloping south-eastwards to its tip at Ras Muhammad. There were ports, connected by coastal roads, along each gulf to meet the needs of the maritime traffic between Egypt and Arabia. Inland communication between these points is not easy. In the north the steep mountains of Et Tih and El Egma effectively bar the way. To the south of the mountains vast sandy wastes make movement by man or beast very difficult. Still farther south are the granite mountains, exceeding 6,509 feet in height, with only a few tortuous passes along dried-up watercourses overhung by sheer rock face on either side. The trans-desert roads pass through Feiran, the largest of the Sinai oases, and the chief passes run near Jebel Musa, the traditional Mount Sinai.

The Peninsula's chief mineral deposits are to be found in this region, which the Egyptians called the 'Land of Mines'. The trans-desert roads increased in importance of course with the growth of the mining enterprises. Nowadays manganese is exploited in the region, chiefly in the large-scale enterprise at Umm Bogma. In ancient times copper was mined here and, even more important, the greenish turquoise beloved of the ancient Egyptians. In the centre of the mining region stood a great temple dedicated to the Egyptian goddess of mines, Hathor. In this temple at Serabit el Khadem and at the entrance to numerous mines hundreds of inscriptions have been found telling of journeys undertaken to the 'Land of Mines' and invoking the aid of the great Egyptian goddess in various mining enterprises.

Plate 32

Plates 50–52

Not all the inscriptions are in hieroglyphs. Both in the temple and on the walls of some of the mines there are inscriptions in the famous Proto-Sinaitic script. Approximately forty of these latter inscriptions have been discovered so far. Their correct decipherment has still to be settled. However, two facts are beyond dispute: these inscriptions are in alphabetical, not hieroglyphic, characters and are written in a Western Semitic language resembling Pre-Canaanite. These are the oldest alphabetical inscriptions known to us and from them we can trace the evolution of later alphabets via Phoenician–Canaanite. They show that among the workers in these mines of the ancient Egyptians were speakers of a Semitic language written in characters which may be regarded as the progenitor of our modern alphabet. They were inscribed on the quarry walls in approximately the fifteenth century B.C., about two hundred years before the Exodus.

Sinai was a land of transit and as such we read of it in the Bible accounts too. The children of Israel pass through Sinai on their way from Egypt looking towards the Promised Land of Canaan. The Bible represents their forty-year sojourn in the wilderness as a punishment for their weakness and their lack of faith in themselves and their God. But in later generations many of their descendants were to see in this period the golden age of a nation in the making, an era of purity and nobility, when People and God were still close to each other, when Law and Statutes were promulgated and when the scattered tribes were welded into a united nation inspired by an exalted ideal.

With increasing idealization of the era of Sinai, however, the physical landmarks of the territory faded into oblivion. To-day the problem of identifying the route of the Exodus and Mount Sinai itself is one of extraordinary difficulty, far more difficult than any other problem of Palestinian Biblical topography.

The Bible has long lists of places where the children of Israel camped in the desert, but unfortunately the places themselves are nowhere described in any detail, nor are there any topographical features mentioned which might help us in their identification. Admittedly some spots are singled out as having abundance of water or palm trees, but these statements are, obviously, only relatively true, and every oasis in Sinai has some water and some palm trees. On the other hand, the lack of continued settlement in Sinai has certainly led to the original names of most of the oases being forgotten, and it is difficult to trace any connexion between their Biblical names and those by which they are at present known.

The only stations on the Israelites' journey about which, in the light of recent research, there can be no doubts are the first, on the Egyptian border, and the last, or at any rate the northernmost, on the border of Canaan. We shall begin our investigation therefore with these sites, describing in particular the important oasis of Kadesh-barnea, much intensive research on which was carried out in 1956–57, during the Israeli occupation of Sinai.

When the Israelites left Raamses and the land of Goshen to cross the great desert they turned and encamped 'before Pi-hahiroth, between Migdol and the sea, over against Baal-zephon' (Exod. xiv. 2) until they reached the 'Sea of Reeds'. These names, of places on the eastern side of the Nile Delta, are Canaanite, not Egyptian. 'Migdol' occurs in certain Egyptian inscriptions as the name of one of the *Shur Mitzraim* fortresses that guarded the approaches to the desert. The clearest of the geographical descriptions provided by the hieroglyphic inscriptions is to be found in a group of reliefs of the reign of Seti I (*c.* 1300 B.C.), the father of Rameses II, who reigned a generation or two before the Exodus. These reliefs describe a military expedition of Pharaoh's to Canaan and his return to Egypt laden with rich booty. The forts, wells and staging-posts along the short Gaza-Rafiah coastal road to the modern Qantara are enumerated. This vital line of communications was well guarded by the Egyptians, as we learn from these reliefs and other documents, and it was this 'way of the land of the Philistines' which the Israelites avoided 'lest peradventure the people repent when they see war, and they return to Egypt' (Exod. xiii. 17). The most westerly of the staging-posts was Sile, near the modern Qantara, which the reliefs show as having a reedy canal with bridge. From here it was possible to sail to the Nile. The post before Sile is depicted with a fortress. An inscription underneath reads: The Tower of Seti. In a somewhat later document this fortress is called the 'Migdol of Meneptah', grandson of Seti I, the Egyptians frequently ascribing the name of the ruling Pharaoh to a fortress in which their troops were stationed. This site has been identified with considerable certainty with Tell el Heir, five miles north of Sile, between Qantara and Pelusium, in the

Fig. 1

northern sector of the *Shur Mitzraim*. The identification of this 'Migdol of Seti' (or Meneptah) with the Biblical Migdol ('Fortress') cannot be in any doubt, as it is mentioned immediately after Succoth, which was the beginning of the journey, and we are obliged to look for it in the zone of the Egyptian border fortifications. It is unlikely that a name so obviously Canaanite as Migdol would be used by the Egyptians more than once in a given area.

The name 'Baal-zephon' provides additional evidence for this identification and for the identification of the starting point of the Exodus. As we learn from certain documents, this was the name of a temple known to mariners and was later called Zeus Casius. This temple stood on the narrow land-strip bordering Lake Sirbonis to the north. The two names Migdol and Baal-zephon (Heb. *zephon*, 'north'), coming next to one another as they do, and identifiable in various documents as they are, leave no room for doubt that Exod. xiv. 2 refers to this region. Pi-hahiroth, mentioned with them, has not yet been identified, but some scholars consider it, perhaps rightly, to be one of the canals (from the root *hrt* 'to dig') linking the various lakes reaching to the Nile in this region. Also 'Reed Sea' occurs in an

Egyptian document as the name of one of the lakes near Raamses, the ancient capital of Egypt in the northern part of the Delta. 'Reed Sea' could of course refer to any lake, but it is a fact that reeds abounded particularly in the Nile Delta lakes, as Egyptian paintings show.

The fact that all the names mentioned in Exod. xiv. 2 can be identified with sites in the northern Delta cannot be a coincidence, and we are justified in assuming it to be a proven fact that the Exodus began here. It is possible that the Israelites went along the narrow neck of land on which Baal-zephon stood and that the Biblical 'Sea of Reeds' was the present-day Sabkhet el Bardawil (Lake Sirbonis). This salt-water lagoon was formed by one of the Nile estuaries and one can assume that in ancient Egyptian times it was a fresh-water lake with reeds growing on its edges. In any event, the Israelites moved northwards, keeping fairly close to the Egyptian road to Canaan. It is for this reason, no doubt, that the Bible emphasizes that although the 'way of the land of the Philistines' was near, and the Israelites' immediate destination was Canaan, they did not take the path of the famous Way itself. Had the Israelites intended to begin their journey by going south first, it is clear that they would not have been able to travel along the Way, which takes a different direction altogether. It is very difficult to-day to follow the more southerly part of the Way, as this narrow coastal strip is covered with shifting sand dunes rising to a great height and completely burying numerous ancient remains. This is undoubtedly the chief reason why up to the present day not a single one of the wells or forts described in the Egyptian inscriptions and reliefs has been discovered between Qantara and El Arish.

An instructive picture of the whole region is afforded near Sheikh Zuweid, midway between Rafiah and El Arish. Sheikh Zuweid itself is a white-domed Moslem sacred tomb near which live Beduin who are in process of changing their nomadic way of life to one of permanent settlement. The tomb is three miles from the coast, roughly at the end of the sand strip. Near it an ancient tell has been found, Tell Abu Suleima, which was partly dug by Sir Flinders Petrie. The name of the site thus dug up has been published as Anthedon, but there is no basis whatever for such an identification. The excavations showed that the settlement was founded c. the fourteenth century B.C. and lasted till Roman times.

From here we went over the sand dunes towards the sea for about a mile-and-a-quarter, where we found another tell—Tell Junein. At first we thought we had found a complete settlement, but we soon realized that what we could see was only the summit of the ancient site; all the lower slopes were completely covered by sand up to a great height. We were able to gather rich material from the Hellenistic, Roman and Byzantine periods, including a few Nabataean sherds. We felt we were standing on the remains of a once-great and prosperous city that was gradually sinking in a sea of sand, and that within the near future it would be completely submerged by the yellow flood. We carried on right up to the beach itself to find yet a third mound, Tell el Sheikh. Here we found some pottery, chiefly Roman, and also a number of complete jars bearing Latin inscriptions.

Plate 2

Plates 1, 4–6

It is obvious that Tell Junein and Tell el Sheikh were two sister-townships, one near the *via maris*, close to the edge of the sandy strip, and the second a seaport on the shore itself. They are probably identifiable as Bitulion, which is marked on the Madeba map as lying between Rafiah and Rhinocorura (El Arish). It was the see of a bishop, and is mentioned in many Byzantine sources. According to Theodosius Betulia was twelve miles from Rafiah, which fits Tell Junein exactly.

Similar pairs of tells, one some distance from the edge of the sea shore on the edge of the sandy strip, and the second right on the shore, occur elsewhere in this region, in Rafiah and Gaza, for example. In all the coastal tells we investigated south of Gaza we found only Hellenistic and post-Hellenistic material, whereas in most of the inland tells we found sherds from the Late Bronze Age and after. This shows that the ancient 'way of the land of the Philistines' kept some distance from the shore, on the edge of the sandy strip, and it is doubtful whether there was any seaport south of Gaza at this period. It was not till the Nabataeans came and began to import precious merchandise from Arabia into the Roman-Hellenistic world that a few seaports were established south of Gaza. It seems possible, therefore, that the Israelites' journey began from the sea shore itself, north-west of the nearby 'way of the land of the Philistines'. They would not have been able to reach Canaan keeping to the 'Way' itself. Gaza was the centre of Egyptian rule in Canaan at the time. It is mentioned in a number of Egyptian documents as the 'City of Canaan' simply; south of it, strung out along Wadi Gaza—perhaps the 'brook Besor' (I Sam. xxx. 9)—a chain of powerful Canaanite strongholds blocked their path, the westernmost of which was the formidable Tell el Ajjul, probably the ancient Beth Aglaim. The Israelites never reached the gates of Gaza at all, in spite of the fact that at the beginning of their journey they were in a direct line of approach to Canaan. We can be certain that they took the first opportunity of getting away from the neighbourhood of the 'way of the land of the Philistines' to make a detour east of the 'Way to Shur', which led direct to the Negeb, to the region of Beersheba and the land of Gerar by the traditional route, used long before by the Patriarchs in their journeyings to and fro between Canaan and Egypt. Along this road they would have to pass near Kadesh-barnea, the largest oasis on the Canaanite border, and this region became the most important and the most hallowed of the Israelites' resting places in the years of their wandering in the wilderness.

Both the name (the Hebrew root *kdš* signifies 'holy') and the various statements in the Bible about the region testify to Kadesh-barnea's being a hallowed centre for the Israelites. Traditionally the families of Moses and Aaron the priest were buried here, Miriam died and was buried here, and the death of Aaron himself occurred not far off, in Mount Hor. The place is also called the 'Waters of Meribah ("strife") of Kadesh' or 'Ain Mishpat' ('the spring of judgement') and it is not unlikely that here were laid the first foundations of Hebrew Law. We know that in the days of the Judges the various Israelite tribes gathered round a central temple, in the manner of the Ancient Greek Amphictyon. In a later period of the Judges' rule this central temple was situated in Shiloh, but previously it had existed in various other places, e.g., Shechem, Gilgal and Beth-el. We have many indications that the Israelites' first Amphictyon was in Kadesh-barnea, where the various tribes assembled and welded themselves into a nation before they entered Canaan. The Bible stresses that the Israelites stayed in Kadesh-barnea, for a considerable time (Deut. i. 46), presumably because it was here that the joint religious and judicial institutions of the tribes were concentrated. One fact emerges clearly and indisputably from the Biblical accounts: Kadesh-barnea was the base for the invasion of Canaan. From here the messengers were sent to spy out the land. From here the first attempt of invasion was made, in spite of the opposition of Moses, and encountered stiff resistance from the king of Arad in the Negeb. The Israelites were decisively defeated at Hormah (Num. xiv. 45; Deut. i. 44), although according to another tradition it was the Israelites who defeated the Canaanites at Hormah (Num. xxi. 1–3). The name Arad has been preserved down to our own day in the great Tell Arad which is at the south-eastern extremity of the great chain of tells in the Negeb. Evidently the king of Arad led a confederation of the Canaanite cities of the Negeb, and it would seem that he succeeded in repulsing the Israelites' first assault wave. Hormah is probably Tell el Milh which is south-west of Arad, east of Beersheba, but this is not certain. But whatever the result of the first battle with the Negeb Canaanites, it is clear that this first attempt to reach Beersheba and Mount Hebron—as in the times of the Patriarchs—was a failure owing to strong resistance by the powerful Canaanite cities in this region. The Israelites continued to wander in the wilderness for a generation—'So ye abode in Kadesh many days' (Deut. i. 46). When their chance came to conquer the territory of Sihon, King of the Amorites in Transjordan, we find them massed once more at their base in Kadesh-barnea. From here messengers were sent to the kings of Edom and Moab to ask for the Israelites to be allowed to pass through their territory, and from here they eventually began the long journey 'to compass the land of Edom' (Num. xxi. 4).

The site of Kadesh is not in doubt. In addition to the verses quoted above which describe it indirectly as being on the borders of Canaan and Edom, there is the precise description of the Canaanite-Judaean borders in Num. xxxiv. 4, and Josh. xv. 3 according to which Kadesh was situated between the south shore of the Dead Sea and the River of Egypt (Wadi el Arish). Its general position, therefore, in the region of the springs and oases to the south of Nitzana is not in doubt. One of these oases, Ain Qadeis, seems even to have kept the ancient name, Kadesh. In spite of the similarity of name, however, both early and modern research has shown that the most important centre of the region was in Ain el Qudeirat, twelve miles north of Ain Qadeis. Why the name Kadesh was preserved in a small oasis twelve miles away from the main centre of the region has yet to be explained.

Ain el Qudeirat is the richest spring in northern Sinai. It flows deep down between two mountain ranges, broadening out on its downward course, and irrigating now as in ancient times a fertile valley. The traveller who suddenly finds himself at the entrance to this valley-garden after hours spent in the pitiless desert sun feels himself uplifted at the sight of these lush green fields. Ain el Qudeirat does not convey the impression of an isolated desert oasis, but of a fruitful valley where all things flourish and where an appreciable number of people can find ample sustenance.

Plates 10, 11

It is not surprising therefore that Kadesh-barnea (as we shall now call Ain el Qudeirat) and the surrounding district abound in ancient remains. In the centre of the valley, and dominating it, a small tell stands out in sharp relief. This tell was discovered before the First World War by Woolley and Lawrence, who carried out a small trial dig on it and published the results in their book, *The Wilderness of Zin*. They were able to reconstruct the plan of an interesting fortress surrounded by a double (casemate) wall. The fortress was laid out in a rectangle, with a tower at each corner and in the middle of each wall. The plan of the fortress, which resembles that of fortresses discovered in excavations in Gibeah of Saul near Jerusalem and in Azekah in the Shefela, as well as the sherds lying in the fortress and on its slopes, leave no room for doubt that it was built in the period of the Divided Kingdom. Its erection indicates clearly the importance attributed to Kadesh-barnea by the kings of Judah.

Plate 15

Fig. 13

Needless to say, Kadesh-barnea particularly attracted the attention of those Israeli scholars who were able to investigate it in the brief period following the Sinai campaign. They discovered many additional remains at Ain el Qudeirat and its environs, and re-investigated the fortress in the centre of the valley.

The finds in the region of Kadesh-barnea belong to the periods of three great civilizations whose remains have been preserved in settlements throughout the Negeb and Sinai: the beginning of the Middle Bronze Age, the period of the Kingdom of Judah, and the Nabataean-Roman-Byzantine period.

Remains of a wave of settlement across the length and breadth of the Negeb have been discovered dating from the first stage of the Middle Bronze Age, sometimes referred to as the Patriarchal period (twenty-first to nineteenth centuries B.C.). This wave was part of the colonization of the Amorites, who had spread over the whole of the Fertile Crescent. They had close relations at this time with the Egyptian Middle Kingdom, which exercised suzerainty over parts of Palestine.

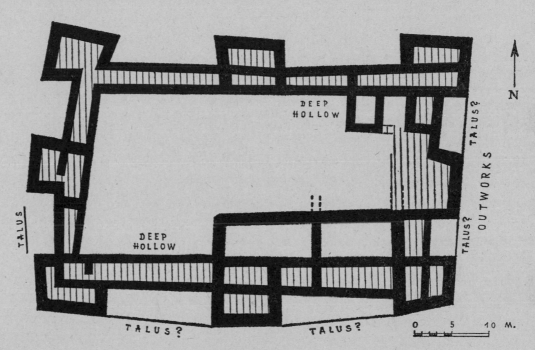

Fig. 13. The Israelite fortress at Ain el Qudeirat (after Woolley and Lawrence)

No doubt these relations helped the semi-nomadic Amorites in their settlement of the Negeb, although we have insufficient historical or archaeological evidence as yet for the understanding of this settlement, its causes and its history. At the entrance to the wadi of Ain el Qudeirat and on all the surrounding hill-tops Beno Rothenberg and others have found building remains dating from this period as well as typical pottery.

Plates 19, 20, 89

The remains are mostly of courtyards, at some distance from each other, conveying the impression that the country was at peace and that every household could put up its tents and its huts wherever its fancy suggested.

In Kadesh-barnea as throughout the Negeb no remains have been found of the period, lasting roughly a thousand years, dating from the beginning of the second to the beginning of the first pre-Christian millennium, that is to say, the late Canaanite and early Israelite period preceding the United Monarchy.

Traces of the Israelites' stay in Kadesh-barnea even in the thirteenth century B.C., before they entered Canaan, have yet to be found. They will doubtless have been

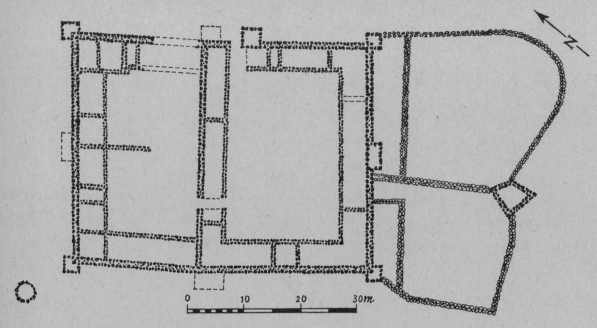

Fig. 14. The fortress of Hurvat Uzzah (Khirbet Ghazza)

buried beneath the later remains and will come to light when more detailed
investigation can be undertaken. In any case, it must be remembered that at this
stage of their history the Israelites were still semi-nomads. As most of their implements were of wood or leather, easily portable, they would pass on their way
leaving little traces of their presence, since these materials cannot be found and
recognized after such a lengthy span of time. Of pottery, which is the modern
archaeologist's chronological master-key, the Israelites certainly had very little. It
is possible that they brought with them certain primitive kinds of pottery, the date
of which, however, we are still unable to fix with any precision.

Nevertheless, although we cannot say what the oasis looked like in the time of
the Israelite wanderings, we can form a fairly accurate picture of it in the days of
the Judaean kingdom, when it was the military and administrative capital of the
whole region.

A description has already been given of the powerful Israelite fortress in the
middle of the valley, discovered by Woolley and Lawrence. They lacked the
equipment which enables modern archaeologists to differentiate precisely between
sherds of different periods, and so they found difficulty in fixing the date of the
building with greater accuracy. Some have attributed it to the reign of David or
Solomon in the tenth century, others ante-dated it to the end of the eleventh
century, in the reign of Saul, basing their view on the similarity of the lay-out of the
fortress and that of Saul's own fortress in Gibeah of Saul.

Our recent investigation of the site brought to light numbers of sherds which can
be assigned only to Iron Age II, that is to say, to the ninth century at the earliest.
Moreover, other sherds were discovered dating from the return to Zion after the
Babylonian exile—one even bore the remains of a Hebrew character—showing that
Jews came back here at the time of the Return and even rebuilt the fortress. The
evidence for not assigning the fortress to a date earlier than the reign of one of the
ninth-century kings of Judah has been strengthened by the writer's discovery in
1957 of a similar fortress, Hurvat Uzzah (Khirbet Ghazza) in the north-east
corner of the Negeb.

Fig. 14

The general plan of the fortress of Hurvat Uzzah is very similar to that of Ain el Qudeirat, both in the casemate walls and in the eight towers at the corners and centres of the walls. In spite of careful searching we failed to find any sherds earlier than the ninth century at Hurvat Uzzah. The question immediately arose whether both buildings were not key fortifications guarding the routes to the Negeb at the time of the Kingdom of Judah. Hurvat Uzzah guarded the approach to Edom and to the Araba, and the fortress of Kadesh-barnea guarded the Darb el Shur leading to Egypt and its branch road leading to Eilat. Both were vital strongholds for the defence of the Negeb and the southern regions of Judah.

It is interesting to note that although no further remains from this period have been discovered in the valley of Ain el Qudeirat, some have come to light on the hill-tops on each side of the valley. It is quite possible that this is more than a mere coincidence, a point to which we shall return later. On the northern hill-top a second, smaller fort was discovered which guarded the approach to the oasis from the hills. This fort may be of earlier date, perhaps tenth century, that is to say of the reign of David and Solomon, but our knowledge of the region's pottery is as yet insufficient to enable us to be definite on this point.

On the other hand, another large Israelite fortress has now been discovered, not in Ain el Qudeirat, but in the neighbourhood of the small oasis of Ain Qadeis.

Plate 16

This fortress stands on the ridge of hills north of Ain Qadeis, about two miles from the spring. It had escaped notice by previous investigators who had explored the valley only. Our attention was drawn to it in the course of interpretation of an air photograph of the region. We could see plainly a large circular fort not marked on the maps and we decided to examine it on the ground. We walked about ten miles from Ain el Qudeirat. On the way we passed many remains relating to settlements of the periods already mentioned, but we had no time to examine them in detail. In all the wadis we passed we saw ancient terraces, perfectly constructed and used to a certain extent by the Beduin even now in the agriculture they occasionally

Plate 13

practise. A Byzantine settlement which we found near the terraces showed clearly that they belong in their present form to the Roman-Byzantine period, when every plot of ground with access to an adequate water supply was cultivated to the limit.

As we ascended the hills of Ain Qadeis we saw our objective ahead of us. At first we were convinced that we had here some late structure, for we saw that part of the walls were still standing, in places even reaching to a height of about six feet. To our surprise, however, we found on reaching the fort that we were looking at one of the most interesting remains of the Israelite period in the whole region.

There had never been any settlement here; only the fort that could be seen from far and wide, dominating not only the gorge below, but the whole plain extending from Ain el Qudeirat to Ain Qadeis, which it guarded against attack from the south. From here roads lead not only to the two springs of El Qudeirat and Qadeis; there is also an important road leading to the northern Negeb via Bir Hafir, along the whole length of which strongholds and watchtowers from the Israelite period have been discovered. From hereabouts, too, ran the ancient road to Elath, along which came the four kings of the north when they returned from 'El-paran which is by the wilderness'—probably Elath bordering on the wilderness of Paran—to 'En-mishpat, which is Kadesh' (Gen. xiv. 6, 7). The fortress of Ain Qadeis, as we shall now designate it, commanded all these roads and was no doubt a key position, the most outlying in the network of frontier forts erected by the kings of Judah to guard against attack from the Sinai desert. *continued on page 137*

THE AWE-INSPIRING granite peaks at the southern tip of the Sinai peninsula seem to form a gigantic clenched fist of God proclaiming: Here!

The ever-changing, ever-deepening colours of the mountains in this part of Sinai, alike of the Nubian sandstone mountains in the northern section of the range and of the granite peaks in the south, invest this indescribably beautiful region with an aura of sanctity, and one can well believe that here God appeared to Moses.

Copper and turquoise miners of old; travellers who crossed the Peninsula from many lands; pilgrims, merchants and soldiers—all left inscriptions to their gods or to themselves, recording the rigours of their journey, on the soft striated hills by the side of the principal caravan routes: in Wadi Mukattab, Wadi Feiran and, further east, in Wadi Taba, Wadi Umm Sideira and elsewhere. In Serabit el Khadem and in Wadi Maghara are stelae commemorating the daring mining enterprises of ancient Egypt and praising her reigning Pharaohs. Here too were found inscriptions in early Hebrew characters.

Jewish tradition was never greatly concerned with the identification of Sinai's 'holy places'. To the Jews in exile Sinai, like Jerusalem, was not of this world. Christian and Moslem pilgrims, however, sought the 'Mountain of God' for centuries. Jebel Serbal and Jebel Musa, Jebel Katherina and Ras Safsafa were all at one time or another claimed as 'Mount Sinai'.

Israeli scholars, who explored the Peninsula in the brief period of Israeli occupation, likewise came to experience a holiness pervading Sinai's mountains, and they tend to believe that it was in this region that the Israelites encamped when the Law was given.

RAS SAFSAFA 49

A peak that 'dwells apart' in the southern Sinai mountain chain is Ras Safsafa, near the monastery of St Catherine. Dr Robinson, the famous Sinai explorer, considered this to be the Biblical Mount Sinai. It lies 6,739 feet above sea-level and about 1,870 feet above the plain of El Raha, conjectured by many to be the region where the six hundred thousand children of Israel heard the thunders and lightnings of the Divine Revelation.

From St Catherine's a path called 'Jethroe's Road' goes up to the summit of Ras Safsafa. It is a very difficult climb which only a few people have accomplished. It is interesting to note that in popular Jewish art it is Ras Safsafa which appears as Mount Sinai. A mural in the former 'Chorva' synagogue, no longer standing, in the Old City of Jerusalem depicted Mount Sinai in the likeness of Ras Safsafa.

ADORATION 50

A drawing of an Egyptian at work or praying, engraved on a rock-face near the cave of Sopd in the sanctuary of Serabit el Khadem. Next to it is a ten-line dedication to an unknown king of the 19th–20th dynasty.

50

51

54

55

51, 52 SERABIT EL KHADEM: STELE COMMEMORATING ANKHRENI, SERVANT OF AMENEMHET III

One of the most important and interesting sites in the Sinai peninsula is the famous Egyptian temple of Serabit el Khadem in the turquoise mining area of the southern mountainous region. Extensive ruins have been preserved which bear a remarkable resemblance to the Canaanite (MB I) buildings found in the Negeb and in central Sinai: stone circles 13–20 feet in diameter with a large upright stone inserted somewhere in the wall. Still earlier remains have also been found (Dr Field, 1948) in the mining region in the vicinity of the temple: Chalcolithic and Early Bronze flint implements.

The Egyptian temple dates from the 19th century B.C. Numerous stones are inscribed in hieroglyphs with eulogies of the Egyptian kings and of the goddess of the place, Hathor, 'she of the cow's ears'. The engraving on the stele shown in the illustration reads: '[the god's treasurer], the intendant, governor of Lower Egypt, Ankhreni, true of voice. He says: O you who live and who are upon earth, officials of the king, courtiers of the palace who may come to this country—Give praise in exalting the might of the kings; extol [the king], behold what has happened for him. The hills lead to what is in them . . .'. [From Gardiner-Peet Černy, *Inscriptions of Sinai*, I, p. 114). This stele was set up in the reign of Amenemhet III, *c.* 1,800 B.C.

Serabit el Khadem is of particular interest, as among the workers in the mines were slaves who had been captured in Canaan. These slaves wrote inscriptions on the rock-walls of the mines in the Canaanite tongue of the 15th century B.C., and in the Proto-Sinaitic script, representing a transitional stage between the Egyptian hieroglyphic and the Canaanite Hebrew script of the end of the second millennium B.C.

53 VIEW FROM THE SUMMIT OF JEBEL MUSA

It is Jebel Musa which Christian tradition identifies with Mount Sinai. It is about 7,370 feet high. On the mountain top a small recently-built Christian church stands next to the ruins of a mosque. There is a magnificent view of the greater part of the Peninsula from here. On the northern horizon stretches the plain of Et Tih.

54 IN WADI FEIRAN

Wadi Feiran is one of the largest and most famous wadis in Sinai. It is 81 miles long and begins in the region of Jebel Musa, where it is called Wadi el Sheikh. The tree in the foreground is an acacia, the typical desert tree of Sinai.

EL MEKHARET, THE TELL IN THE OASIS OF FEIRAN 55

Feiran boasts the chief oasis in Sinai, one of the wonders of the Peninsula. In the heart of the bleak and forbidding granite mountains a green parkland suddenly comes into view: over 6 miles of date-palm groves, tamarisks, reeds, rushes and other vegetation, with a small parkling stream to delight the eye, artesian wells and even a petrol engine to draw up the water. The inhabitants are Beduin.

In the middle of the wadi, near the junction of Wadi Feiran's tributaries, stands a sizeable tell with the remains of a monastery and many other ruins. We know from several sources that this was the site of a Byzantine town inhabited by Christians under their bishop. Generations of travellers and scholars have seen in the oasis of Feiran the Biblical Rephidim of the Exodus. Dr Y. Aharoni, however, identifies Feiran with the Biblical Paran.

The remains of the Byzantine monastery can be seen on the hill in the middle ground of the photograph.

TOMB OF NEBI SALIH IN WADI EL SHEIKH 56

Wadi el Sheikh, a tributary of Wadi Feiran, is the site of the main road-junction of southern Sinai. In the broad plain of the valley is the tomb of Nebi Salih. In its construction it is typical of the resting-places of the desert sheikhs: a whitewashed chamber with a domed roof. Nearby runs the road leading from the Gulf of Suez in the west to Dhahab on the coast of the Gulf of Eilat (Aqaba) in the east. Many roads from the north meet at this point, too, and from here the main St Catherine's road continues south.

The Beduin consider the tomb of Sheikh el Nebi Salih to be the most sacred in Sinai. In the spring they hold a great festival near the tomb, with camel races, dancing and sacrifices. The festival is marked by a feature that is not usual among the Beduin: the women and children of the tribe take part, too. The Sinai Beduin identify Nebi Salih with the Salih mentioned in the Koran. Near Ramleh in Israel, too, the local Arabs point to the 'tomb of Nebi Salih'.

JEBEL SERBAL 57

The photograph was taken from Wadi Feiran. Jebel Serbal, which rises to about 6,825 feet, is called *El Medahawe* ('The Tower of Light') in Arabic, because this peak is the first to catch the light of dawn, when it is bathed in a delicate shade of pink. Both on its slopes and near the summit many early inscriptions have been cut into the rock-face. Jebel Serbal stands out in lone splendour from the other, higher peaks in the region. Viewed from Wadi Feiran, in particular, it rises glorious in majesty; small wonder that many travellers have identified it with the 'Mountain of God'.

Fig. 15

Plate 18

Plate 90

The fortress of Ain Qadeis, like that of Kadesh-barnea, has casemate walls. It is only a little smaller than the fortress of Kadesh-barnea, but in contrast to the latter's rectangular shape, it is circular, or rather oval, to conform to the configuration of the hill on which it stands. It is unlikely that the two fortresses were built at the same time.

The main gate in the south wall of the Ain Qadeis fortress is clearly discernible. The wall near the gate has been preserved to a greater height than elsewhere and the corner-part is an excellent example of Israelite building style. The large blocks of stone are roughly cut and are laid 'stretcher' and 'header' alternating.

After some time spent in careful search we found an appreciable number of Iron Age sherds. Some of them can be assigned approximately to the ninth century, as they are like those found at Kadesh-barnea, but others are quite different, unlike any found at Kadesh, and are difficult to date. These latter were hand-made from coarse clay; the hand-marks are still visible in many places. Most of these sherds were from simple jars finished off with round lips and no necks. This primitive pottery is not found in Palestine in the Iron Age, and we can assume therefore that it was used in the Negeb and Sinai for a limited period, which makes it difficult to assign its precise date.

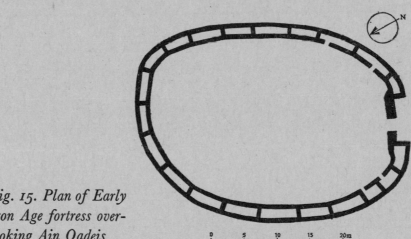

Fig. 15. Plan of Early Iron Age fortress overlooking Ain Qadeis

Nevertheless, there can be no doubt that it belongs to the Iron Age, more precisely to the tenth to ninth centuries and perhaps even earlier. Similar pottery was discovered by Professor Glueck in his excavations of Ezion-gaber, the results of which have unfortunately not yet been published. The writer continued looking for this pottery among sherds collected from other sites in the Negeb and found an appreciable quantity of it in sherds brought from the mining centres in the area of Nahal Timnah. It is known that mining began in this region in the time of Solomon at least, which strengthens the attribution of these sherds to the tenth century. Also, in the fortress of Ain Qadeis we found a thin rim of a carinated bowl or chalice, which cannot possibly be later than the tenth century and may well be earlier.

Has our discovery of the Ain Qadeis fortress affected the traditional identification of Kadesh-barnea with Ain el Qudeirat? Although the Ain Qadeis fortress seems somewhat earlier than that of Ain et Qudeirat, it dates in all probability from the time of the monarchy, and we can make no inferences from it regarding the encampments of the Israelites during the period of their wanderings in the thirteenth century B.C. Obviously the most important settlement in the whole region would have to be in Ain el Qudeirat, but in the time of the monarchy the other springs were utilized too, and the chief border-stronghold was erected near the most southerly of the springs. It is possible that the whole region was called Kadesh-barnea at certain periods of its history and the old name retained in the nomenclature of one of the springs, in this case the southernmost, though not the most important.

Similarly it may be conjectured that the fortress of Ain Qadeis is identical with the Biblical Hazar-addar. In the list of places encountered by Shishak, king of Egypt, in his invasion of Palestine after the death of Solomon, we read for the first time of *Hagars* in the Negeb. Professor Mazar has shown that this refers to frontier and highway fortresses, from the Hebrew root *hgr*, that is to say 'to surround with a girdle, a fortification'. Our fortress was doubtless one of these girdles. The word '*Hagar*' does not occur in the Bible, and we may conjecture that the word '*Hazer*' (*hsr*, 'courtyard') takes its place, as in the frequent mention of '*Hazar-*' (the 'construct state' of '*Hazer*') in the list of towns falling to the lot of Simeon (Josh. xix. 3, 5) and in the enumeration of towns in the Negeb of Judah (Josh. xv. 23, 25, 27, 28). The chief '*Hazer*' in the district of Kadesh-barnea was Hazar-addar, as may be seen from the Biblical description of the borders of Canaan. The boundary of Canaan stretched from the region of the Dead Sea: 'and the going forth thereof shall be from the *south* of (*sic*—the A.V. 'to' is inaccurate here) Kadesh-barnea, and shall go on to Hazar-addar, and pass on to Azmon: And the border shall fetch a compass from Azmon unto the river of Egypt' (Num. xxxiv. 4, 5). The southern border of the tribe of Judah is similarly described in Josh. xv. 3, except that there the name Hazar-addar is split up into two: Hezron and Adar. It would seem that we have here the description of the network of fortifications that was strung out *south* of Kadesh-barnea, and based on the fortress of Ain Qadeis, the Biblical Hazar-addar.[1]

The border-forts of Judah, then, lay to the south of Ain el Qudeirat. Nevertheless Ain el Qudeirat was the chief centre of the whole region, and so in the reign of the kings of Judah it was here that the main fortification was built, not in a strategical position commanding one of the heights, but in the valley and near the spring, guarding only the valley of Qudeirat, Kadesh-barnea, itself. This shows clearly the key significance of Ain el Qudeirat and the importance that was attached to securing control of its abundant springs and fertile valley.

The most striking remnant of antiquity in Kadesh-barnea, apart from the tell itself, is a long wall surrounding all the upper part of the valley. It had already been noticed by Woolley and Lawrence, but they were unable to ascertain its function and date.

Plates 10, 17

Nothing is more difficult than assigning a date to a wall, particularly when, as in this case, it is not connected with any particular settlement. However, although we are still in the dark about the date of the Qudeirat wall, it does provide interesting material for a number of conjectures regarding the special function of Kadesh-barnea.

For what purpose was the wall built? In reality it is not so much a wall as a carefully constructed stone fence about five feet high and more than three feet thick. It is constructed of rough stones taken from the neighbourhood, laid in slapdash courses. It is not strong enough to serve any defensive purpose, and cannot have been built with any such aim in mind. In the south it runs along the crest of

[1] See Beno Rothenberg "Cadès Barné" in *Bible et Terre Sainte*, 1960, pp. 4-14.

Plate 10 the hill, but in the north it crosses the tactically useless lower parts of the sloping side of the valley.

Did it serve as a fence for fields under cultivation, like the many fences in the Negeb that enclose wadis within which are to be found cultivated fields and ancient terraces? Hardly, one would think, since the wall of Kadesh-barnea, though not strong enough for defensive purposes, is much stouter than these Negeb fences and, moreover, at many points it is far distance from the area under cultivation in the valley.

Nor is the configuration of the wall suitable for storing water or preventing floods. It does not follow any fixed topographical line, and descends abruptly to the valley. To the east both arms of the wall descend directly towards the new dam, which without doubt stands on the same spot where the early dams were built, too, in the narrowest part of the wadi. To the west the wall runs down directly towards the valley from both sides. Whether it crossed the valley itself at this point there is now no means of telling, as the part of the wall that extended into the valley was completely destroyed.

The nearest analogous structure is the wall surrounding the 'Sacred Mountain', which was discovered between Beerotaim (Birein) and Bir Hafir, about eight miles north of Kadesh-barnea, by Professor Nelson Glueck's expedition. It resembles the Qudeirat wall in construction and dimensions, and like that wall seems to fulfil no practical function. It is built on the uplands of a fairly prominent mountain west of Bir Hafir, near the junction of the roads leading from the Negeb to Eilat and Sinai. The wall surrounds the greater part of the mountain but, again, clearly cannot serve any defensive purpose. At places the wall runs yards away from the crest of the mountain and there are four large openings in it; an opening in each direction: north, south, east, west. It is clear also that the wall could serve no agricultural or habitation purpose, for the mountain itself was never cultivated or inhabited.

Nelson Glueck called this mountain, rightly I think, the 'Sacred Mountain'. Inside the wall are two large circles, with smaller circles of stone inside them. In many places there are also small heaps of stones, seemingly memorial cairns. On the basis of the pottery he discovered on the site Glueck concluded that at all times when there was a settled or semi-nomadic population in the region the wall marked a central burying place and sacred mountain.

Glueck's conclusion seems plausible, and we may conclude that the function of the wall was to limit and bound the sacred place. We may compare what is said about Mount Sinai in Exod. xix. 12: 'And thou shalt *set bounds* to the people [in the Samaritan version: to the mountain] round about saying, Take heed to yourselves, that ye go not up into the mount', and xix. 23: 'And Moses said unto the Lord: The people cannot come up to mount Sinai: for thou chargedst us, saying, *Set bounds about the mount*, and sanctify it.'

It is possible therefore that, just as was the wall of the 'Sacred Mountain', so the wall of Kadesh-barnea was built to 'set bounds' about a spot which was hallowed, as both the meaning of the name 'Kadesh' and the Biblical verses we have cited would indicate.

At what period was the wall built? The fact that we read of Kadesh-barnea's holiness in the Bible is not a proof that it was not built in post Biblical times, as traditions of holiness are handed down from generation to generation, from age to age. Glueck assumes that the wall of the 'Sacred Mountain' was built in the Nabataean period, without being able to bring any evidence in support of his assertion. In my view we have grounds for assuming that the wall of Kadesh-barnea was built in the Israelite period.

If the assumption that the Kadesh-barnea wall was erected to surround and delimit 'hallowed soil' is correct, then it follows that the settlements or buildings contemporaneous with the construction of the wall must have been more or less at the centre of the wall. It is true there are Nabataean-Roman-Byzantine remains, e.g., dams, canals, reservoirs, scattered about the whole valley, but we have now succeeded in discovering, in addition, a large, central settlement which, from the evidence of its sherds, existed from the Nabataean to the end of the Byzantine period. This settlement lay north-west of the Israelite fortress, on the slope of a spur on the north side of the valley. Here, where the valley broadens out, are the most fertile fields of the oasis, watered by its bubbling spring. The country was at peace and so the settlement could be conveniently sited near the cultivated area, away from the fortress. It was no longer necessary to have regard to military considerations. As in many other settlements, here the Roman-Byzantine settlement was the direct successor of a Nabataean, attested by a quantity of fine, delicate pottery.

The Nabataean settlement had its site in the valley on the same spur of land on which the wall ran down. The part of the wall that extended into the trough of the valley was demolished before it reached the settlement, and it seems very likely that the Nabataeans were responsible for the demolition. On the other hand, a glance at the map on page 34 will show that the Israelite fortress was almost in the precise centre of the wall, by which it is surrounded on all sides.

All we can say with certainty from the archaeological evidence is that the wall is pre-Byzantine in construction. A little above the Nabataean settlement the wall has been demolished in several parts and replaced by square rooms. A brief examination showed that one side of these rooms was formed by a piece of the wall itself, and that the other sides were built with stones taken from parts of the wall which had been demolished. In between each room, then, was a uniform gap in the wall. It is abundantly clear that these rooms are later than the wall itself, and that when they were built the wall itself was no longer used for its original purpose, as whoever was responsible for the rooms had no compunction in breaking up the wall to construct them.

Inside these structures we found Byzantine pottery—so the wall must be pre-Byzantine. There still remains the possibility that it is Nabataean, but we have seen that there was a continuity of Nabataean-Byzantine settlement, which would support the thesis that it is pre-Nabataean too. The excellent state of preservation of the wall in many places does not argue against its antiquity; the fortress of Ain Qadeis, for example, shows how wonderfully suited this dry desert region is to the preservation of antiquities.

However, whether the wall is of Israelite or Nabataean origin, its existence strengthens the case for the identification of Kadesh-barnea with Ain el Qudeirat. If we are right in assuming that the wall bounded a hallowed site in ancient times, then we would expect to find near it remains dating from the period of the Israelite wanderings in the desert. There is a presumption that the small tell on which the Israelite fortress was built would have such remains buried beneath it, but only a large-scale excavation could confirm this. A further presumption is that only communal buildings stood on the hallowed site, which explains perhaps why ancient remains are found all over the area except in the valley itself.

We shall conclude this chapter by briefly considering the question of the identification of Mount Hor, the burying place of Aaron the Priest 'in the sight of all the congregation'.

What do we know about this peak? The account of Aaron's death on top of the mountain shows that it was held to be hallowed soil, traditionally the burying place of Moses' family. Not only Aaron, but Miriam, his and Moses' sister, died and were buried in the region of Kadesh-barnea (Num. xx. 1). Its name, too, probably testifies to its being a place hallowed to God, Hor being a theophoric word—Mount Hor, the mountain of God. The name *Har-el*, 'mountain of God' occurs in the list of Thothmes III and we know of other ancient names in which 'Hor' or 'Har' represents a theophoric element, e.g., Jakob-har and Anath-har.

Mount Hor was the first halting-place on the Israelites' wanderings after Kadesh-barnea (Num. xx. 22; xxxiii. 37). It was on the borders of Edom (Num. xx. 23; xxxiii. 37).

A late tradition identified Mount Hor with Jebel Harun, east of the Araba on the road to Petra, following a mistaken identification of Kadesh-barnea with Rekem-Edom (Petra) which is found as far back as Flavius Josephus and Eusebius. However, the identification of Mount Hor with Jebel Harun is impossible, the latter being in the heart of Edom, far removed from Kadesh-barnea.

Modern opinion identifies Mount Hor with Jebel el Madra, a limestone peak by Maale-Aqrabim, in the centre of the Nahal Zin (Wadi Fikra). Although the mountain is a prominent landmark, no ancient remains have been found on it; neither settlement, nor wall, nor graves. This opinion derives from the premise that the Israelites journeyed from Kadesh-barnea towards the Araba, but a closer examination of the Biblical accounts leaves no doubt that the tradition of Mount Hor is linked with the route from Kadesh-barnea to Arad, for the encounter with the king of Arad is always mentioned immediately after Mount Hor (Num. xxi. 1; xxxiii. 40). The road from Kadesh-barnea to Arad, of course, did not go by way of the Araba. It turned north via Bir Hafir towards Beer Yerucham (Bir Rekhme), as is shown by the Israelite fortresses and watch-towers recently discovered all along the route. The fact that Mount Hor is mentioned as being on the borders of Edom accords with its being not too far from Kadesh-barnea, which also is described as a city on the uttermost border of Edom (Num. xx. 17).

These requirements are all neatly met by the sacred mountain, on the road from Kadesh-barnea to Arad, and close to the former, that was discovered by Glueck's expedition. It is not particularly high, but it stands out from a distance in the great plain between Bir Hafir and Beerotaim (Birein), a plain that abounds in remains of the three periods: Middle Bronze, Israelite and Nabataean-Byzantine; periods during which the Negeb civilization flourished. The wall, the stone circles, the cairns and the sherds scattered here and there all bear witness that for a prolonged period of time it was a holy mountain and a main burying place for the region's inhabitants. We have no certain proof, but it seems to the writer that this mountain must be regarded as one of the most serious candidates for identification with the Biblical Mount Hor. It is interesting to note that Père Abel had suggested looking for Mount Hor in this area, the idea having been suggested to him by the name Wadi Harunia which runs near the mountain. It is not impossible that we have here a tradition corresponding to that which associated Jebel Harun with the mountain on which Aaron died.

II

WELL INFORMED though we may now be about Kadesh-barnea, the great Israelite rallying-point during the Exodus, and its environs, the identification of Mount Sinai is still shrouded in deep mystery. Nevertheless, our investigations have shed new light on the various possibilities and are gradually leading us towards a solution of this problem, too.

The crucial question in considering the problem of identification is: Are we to look for Mount Sinai in the southern or northern part of the Peninsula? The tradition identifying the mountain with Jebel Musa, one of the highest of the granite peaks in southern Sinai, goes back to the Byzantine period. To fit this identification, the route of the Exodus has been taken as describing a great arc proceeding from Egypt southwards by the shore of the Red Sea to Jebel Musa, and then northwards via the coast of the Gulf of Aqaba to Kadesh-barnea.

Plate 53

We know now that this route is not supported by the sources at our disposal. We have already pointed out that the first names mentioned in the Bible before the crossing of the Red Sea—Migdol and Baal-zephon—clearly indicate that the route went north, more or less parallel to the 'way of the land of the Philistines' which was barred to the Israelites. Accordingly, we can no longer be in any doubt that the Israelites' first objective was the region of Kadesh-barnea, which served the Israelite tribes as base throughout all their years of wandering in the desert. This is borne out, to some extent at any rate, by the repeated references to 'three days journey into the desert' which the Israelites made that they might 'hold a feast' and 'sacrifice unto the Lord' (Exod. v. 1-3; xv. 22; Num. xxxiii. 8). The 'three days in the wilderness' were spent by the Israelites in the wilderness of Shur (Exod. xv. 22), on the Egyptian border. It was a hard journey, with neither wells nor oases to lighten the trek, and it took three days for the Israelites to reach their first halting-point: Marah. It is worthy of note that Marah is the subject of a cryptic verse: 'There he made for them a statute and an ordinance (*mishpat*), and there he proved them' (Exod. xv. 25). There are references in a similar vein to Kadesh-barnea, which is called En-mishpat ('the spring of judgement') and 'the water of Meribah ('strife') in Kadesh' (Gen. xiv. 7; Num. xx. 13; xxvii. 14). The western part of the Way to Shur, from the region of Jebel el Maghara to the Bitter Lakes, runs through arid country. Along it no remains of settlements, wells or oases have been discovered. It was probably this tract of land which the Israelites referred to as 'three days journey'.

Plate 33

We know, then, that the Israelites' first objective was Kadesh-barnea. Here they 'abode many days'; from here they launched all their attempted invasions of Canaan, and here was their hallowed place of assembly all through the years of their wandering in the wilderness. Are we not obliged to assume, then, that the holy Mount of Sinai, too, which according to tradition the Israelites reached on their way to Kadesh-barnea, lay in the same region? A number of scholars hold this view. They consider that of the mountains in the region the one most likely to have been Mount Sinai is Jebel el Halal, which rises about twenty-five miles to the west of Kadesh-barnea and is clearly visible from the Kadesh heights. Of course, this is only one of the peaks that might lay claim to the title, for in this region a number of mountain ranges rise with dramatic suddenness from the extensive plain; Jebel Libni and Jebel el Maghara, to name two, each resembling the other!

In any case, an analysis of the relevant Biblical verses reveals many difficulties. We read in the Book of Exodus that the Israelites journeyed from the *Sea of Reeds* to the *Wilderness of Shur*. After travelling for three days they reached *Marah*, whence they proceeded to *Elim*, a blissful spot where were 'twelve wells of water, and three score and ten palm trees' (Exod. xv. 22–27). According to this tradition it was not the journey to Mount Sinai but the journey from the *Sea of Reeds* to the Israelites' first staging-post, that lasted three days. 'And they took their journey from Elim, and all the congregation of the children of Israel came unto the wilderness of Sin, which is between Elim and Sinai' (Exod. xvi. 1).

The Bible has various names for the great wilderness which to-day we call by the name of the Sinai peninsula; five, if we include the southern part of the Negeb: the Wilderness of Zin, The Wilderness of Paran, the Wilderness of Shur, the Wilderness of Sin and the Wilderness of Sinai. There is no doubt that the *Wilderness of Shur* is the region bordering Egypt, near the Shur Mitzraim ('Wall of Egypt'), through which the Biblical 'Way of Shur' passed; cf. the frequent occurrence of phrases like 'Unto Shur that is before Egypt' (Gen. xxv. 18; I Sam. xv. 7) and 'As thou goest to Shur, even unto the land of Egypt' (I Sam. xxvii. 8).

The *Wilderness of Zin* stretches from the north and north-east to Kadesh-barnea; the border of Canaan is described as 'From the wilderness of Zin along by the coast of Edom' (Num. xxxiv. 3). The spies went up from Kadesh-barnea: 'And they searched the land from the Wilderness of Zin unto Rehob, as men come to (*lebo*) Hamath' (Num. xiii. 21). Even Kadesh-barnea itself is sometimes described as being in the Wilderness of Zin (Num. xxvii. 14; xxxiii. 36). However, according to other passages it was situated in the Wilderness of Paran (Num. xiii. 3, 26). The consensus of opinion is that the Wilderness of Paran is the region south and south-east of Kadesh-barnea, which was more or less on the border of the two desert zones. We shall return to this later.

The Wilderness of Sin and of Sinai are not mentioned in connexion with Kadesh-barnea. From the Wilderness of Sinai the Israelites journeyed to the Wilderness of Paran (Num. x. 12; xii. 16). It was only after a long, tiring journey, and after having halted at many other places, that they reached Kadesh-barnea.

If Mount Sinai had been nearer Kadesh-barnea we should have been justified in assuming that this oasis would have been mentioned as one of the stations in the Wilderness of Sinai, or at least as being on the border of the Wilderness of Sinai.

The account in Exodus goes on to relate that the Israelites wandered from the Wilderness of Sin to Rephidim, where the great battle with Amalek took place (Exod. xvii. 8–15), and from here they came to the Wilderness of Sinai and camped before the mount (Exod. xix. 2).

There follow the chapters dealing with the statutes and judgements given to Moses and the Israelites. Afterwards it is stated that they travelled through some places in the Wilderness of Paran, till they came to Kadesh-barnea, whence they despatched the spies to Canaan (Num. x–xii).

Apart from these descriptive verses, the Bible gives us a résumé of the stations of the Israelites' journeyings in the wilderness (Num. xxxiii) with a long list of place-names, some of which are not known to us from any other source. Twenty-eight stations are enumerated from 'the sea' (i.e. the Sea of Reeds) to Kadesh-barnea, seven before the Wilderness of Sinai, and the rest after. The 'Reed Sea' of Num. xxxiii. 10, it should be noted particularly, is not the same 'Reed Sea' that is mentioned in Exodus. In that book, the 'Reed Sea' is the Sea that the Israelites crossed over when they left Egypt; the site of the great miracle. In Num. xxxiii. 8, however, the 'Sea' has no epithet attached to it; the verse simply says: 'And [the children of Israel] passed *through the midst of the sea* into the wilderness.' After three days' journey, however, and after the Israelites had left Marah and Elim, we suddenly find: 'And [they] encamped by the Reed Sea. And they removed from the Reed Sea, and encamped in the Wilderness of Sin' (Num. xxxiii. 10–11). It would seem, therefore, that even as far back as the time of the writing and redaction of these verses, which was almost certainly in the time of the monarchy, various traditions concerning the identification of the Reed Sea were extant. We know that as long ago as Solomon the Gulf of Eilat (Aqaba) was known as the Reed Sea, as clearly appears from I Kings ix. 26: 'And king Solomon made a navy of ships in Ezion-gaber, which is besides Eloth, *on the shore of the Reed Sea,* in the land of Edom.' The redactors of Num. xxxiii chose to consider the Reed Sea as one of the stations of the Exodus, and not as being on the Egyptian border. We cannot explain why it is that as far back as the period of the monarchy the name 'Reed Sea' had travelled to the Gulf of Aqaba. At the same time, it is clear that the redactors of Num. xxxiii place the Mount Sinai deep in the south—about twenty stations separate it from Kadesh-barnea—but were their traditions authentic?

There is a further difficulty, in that we are still unable to identify confidently a single one of the long list of stations enumerated in Num. xxxiii. If we could identify even only one place, it would at least be a pointer. It is possible that *Hazeroth* has been preserved in Ain Hasera, about thirty-odd miles north-east of Jebel Musa, but this name occurred frequently in the Negeb and Sinai, and hence can be of but little assistance to us.

In the opening verse of the Book of Deuteronomy the name *Dizahab* appears next to *Hazeroth,* and Burckhardt in his day suggested identifying it with Dhahab, which lies on the coast of the Gulf of Aqaba, east of Jebel Musa, some forty miles south of Eilat. This site has now been well investigated by the writer and by Professor Mazar's expedition. It is the chief settlement on the western coast of the Gulf. The Beduin have groves of date-palms dotting the shore, and stone-fenced vegetable gardens. There is a high water table and the Beduin draw their water from numerous cisterns that have been dug throughout the oasis.

The greater part of the modern settlement is concentrated south of the broad Wadi Dhahab, which issues from the mountains here into the coastal plain. The site of the ancient settlement, however, was on the north bank of the wadi, close to the shore. Here Mazar's expedition found a long mound containing remains of a rectangular building, probably a fortress. Immediately in front of the fortress were numerous stone heaps, in all likelihood the remains of a jetty and harbour in the centre of the oasis, close to the bank of the wadi. We found other buildings to the east of the fortress, as well as sherds, of Nabataean-Roman-Byzantine origin, scattered over an appreciable distance.

Further evidence of the settlement's special importance is provided by a huge cemetery of more than a hundred large mounds covering built graves, *nawamis* in Beduin parlance, and belonging to the same period. These mounds rise for some miles on either side of the wadi to the east. We first noticed them at night, silhouetted against the ridge. Close by one of them we found a quantity of copper slag, showing that in ancient times the precious metal was mined not far away.

It is clear, then, that Dhahab's importance was something more than that of a large desert oasis; it was a main junction of coastal and up-country routes.

continued on page 161

ST CATHERINE'S

'AND HE SAID, Draw not nigh hither: put off thy shoes from off thy feet, for the place whereon thou standest is holy ground' (Exod. iii. 5).

Inspired by this verse, Byzantine monks in the early centuries of the Christian era built chapels for prayer and contemplation amid the southern mountain ranges of Sinai. They even 'found' the Burning Bush in a narrow wadi bed in the region, and here they built themselves a church. Bringing a vivid imagination to bear on the accounts in the Bible, they also located the other traditional sites: Mount Sinai and the Spring of Moses, the path of Moses our Lord and the church of Elijah. They discovered the 'mountain of thunder and lightnings', and the spot where Moses broke the two tablets of stone and the spot where the earth opened her mouth and swallowed up Korah; they found the hill of Aaron and the burial place of the golden calf.

In the sixth century A.D. the Emperor Justinian built the fortress-monastery of St Catherine's to protect the life and property of the numerous monks in the region against attacks by roving bands of desert marauders. St Catherine's has a fine church with a superb antique mosaic (6th–7th centuries), living quarters, libraries, a bakery and a hospice for pilgrims. In the course of time much additional building took place and many alterations were made, and the great courtyard of the monastery became a small town with winding streets, dark narrow passage-ways, kitchen-gardens, and vines overhanging the alleys.

A Christian legend tells of a fair, godly maiden in the city of Alexandria who in the year 307 publicly accused the Emperor Maximinus of idolatry. She was tortured and put to death by the Emperor's order and her body brought by angels to the summit of the mountain near the monastery. Here it was discovered centuries later by the monks, who transferred her bones to the monastery church. Even since, the monastery has been called St Catherine's, after the martyred maid.

The monastery's ancient library is an inexhaustable treasure-house whose great value has only recently come to be appreciated. It has a superb collection of icons, too, many of them painted by monks in the monastery itself.

A small desert tribe, the Jebelia, has its tents in the neighbourhood of the monastery. These people differ in appearance from the other Sinai Beduin tribes. According to legend they are descended from Wallachian slaves who were sent by Justinian to minister to the monks and guard the monastery. Many were killed in the Moslem conquest of the Peninsula and the survivors forced to accept the faith of the Prophet.

At present there are twelve monks living in the monastery; working, praying and attending to the needs of pilgrims.

Viewed from the surrounding peaks the ancient monastery might be a fabulous castle.

THE OLD HOIST AND THE MONKS' LIVING QUARTERS 58

The monastery's old hoist was worked by hand by two monks or servants. The opening in the wall through which visitors were hoisted is about 90 feet above ground level. At one time it was not easy to gain entry. The intending visitor had to arm himself with a letter of recommendation from the Archbishop of Sinai who resided in Cairo, and this letter was closely examined before entry was granted. At the present time the hoist is still used for heavy loads and supplies.

WITHIN THE MONASTERY WALLS 59

The monastery presents the appearance of a typical medieval fortress, with its twisting alleys, and its overcrowded buildings in various styles, constructed of bizarre materials and set down in a confused heap. Among the structures inside the great wall surrounding the fortress-monastery are two wells, a flour mill, an olive press and numerous chapels.

A MONK BY THE MONASTERY WALL 60

In the 6th century Procopius, Justinian's famous secretary, described the life of the monks at St Catherine's as 'a detailed study of death'. This description holds very largely to-day. They observe prolonged periods of self-mortification when they abstain completely from milk, eggs, fish and fats. They spend the greater part of the day in prayer and in light 'household duties'—they clean their own rooms. Their habit is a long black or blue gown fastened by a narrow girdle and a black, high-crowned skull-cap.

ST CATHERINE'S 61

This famous fortified monastery at the foot of Jebel Musa was named after the maid Catherine, who according to an early legend, was martyred for her faith in 307 A.D. The monastery was built by the Byzantine emperor Justinian in the 6th century. The number of monks living in the monastery has varied. In 1957 there were twelve, in addition to the monastery servants drawn from the Jebelia tribe.

Within the fortress-monastery's walls (approximately 279 feet wide by 312 feet long; the height ranges from 33 to 49 feet) is a miniature city with a splendid church, a small mosque (built in 1103), living rooms, bakery, refectory and servants' quarters. The large building on the far side of the monastery in the photograph is of recent construction. It houses the famous library and provides accommodation for tourists and pilgrims. Part of the monastery's gardens are seen on the right.

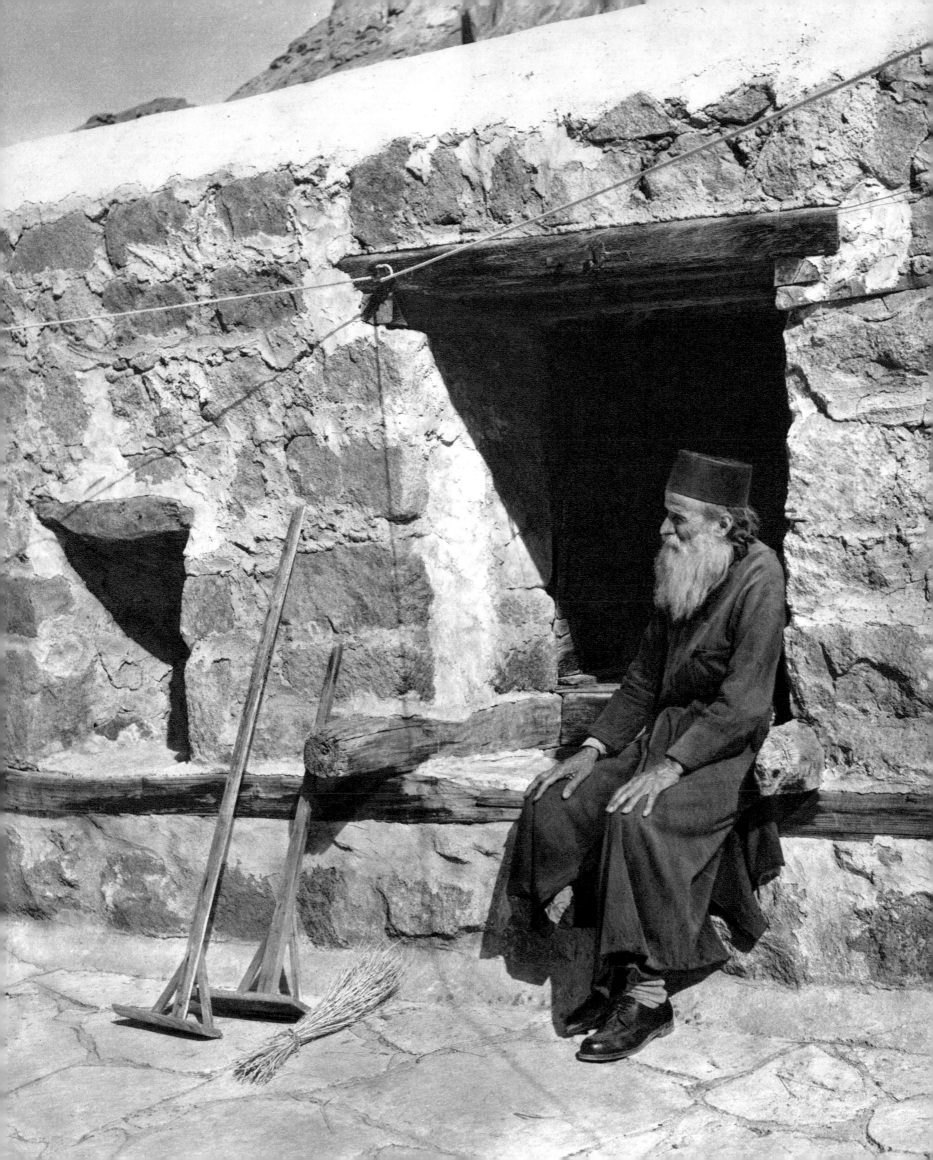

62

63

66

67

68

69

62 FROM THE MONASTERY'S ART COLLECTION

The monastery has a fine collection of icons, some of which were presented, while others were painted by the monks themselves over the centuries. There are very few secular paintings, but this portrait of two mounted knights crusader seems to be one, though the monks will have it that these horsemen are Saints Sergius and Bacchus. The picture dates from the 12th or 13th century. On the back of it is a rather primitive painting of the Virgin Mary.

63 THE BYZANTINE CHURCH

The Church of the Transfiguration in St Catharine's is one of the finest examples of Greek Orthodox architecture. It is richly adored with icons and an abundance of gilt in every nook and corner. According to legend the church was originally built by Helena, the mother of Constantine, in 342, as the Chapel of the Burning Bush, which was reputed to have stood on this site. In 530 the Chapel was enlarged and renamed St Catherine's. The martyr-maid's bones were not brought here till the Middle Ages, when the Church began to attract pilgrims. Among the Church's valuable treasures is a very fine Byzantine mosaic over the apse.

64 IN THE CHARNEL-HOUSE

The monks of St Catherine's still practise the old burial rites. Near the charnel-house, in the beautiful garden just outside the monastery wall, is a small burial-ground, about 15 feet square. Here the monks are laid to rest. About a year after their death the monks' bones are gathered up and added to the heaps of skulls and bones in the charnel-house. Possibly this practice originated when the early monks gathered in the bones of hermits who had died in the rock-caves of the desert. Above the door of the charnel-house is inscribed in Greek the verse from Ecclesiastes: 'Vanity of vanities; all is vanity'.

65 ST STEPHANOS

At the entrance to the charnel-house sits the skeleton of St Stephanos dressed in his habit. St Stephanos was the monastery sexton. He devoted his life to guarding the steps leading to the mountain of Moses and was rewarded at his death with this post of honour by the door of the charnel-house.

ST LUKE DEPICTED IN THE PAGES OF AN ANCIENT NEW 66 TESTAMENT MS

The monastery library, one of the oldest in the world, contains many valuable early MSS. A few years ago an American expedition photographed 3,400 MSS in eleven languages on behalf of the Library of Congress. During their brief stay in the monastery library a group of Hebrew University scholars were able to carry out fruitful research.

One of the library's finest exhibits is this manuscript dating from the end of the tenth century: *Evangeliarium Theodosianum*. According to the monks it was presented to the monastery by the Emperor Theodosius III in 766. The lettering is in gold. The MS has pictures of seven saints, each saint occupying a whole page. The photograph shows St Luke composing his Gospel.

THE LIBRARY 67

The library is of recent construction, and as may be seen from the photograph, presents a marked contrast to the gloomy earlier buildings of the monastery.

BEDUIN GIRL OF THE JEBELIA TRIBE; JEBELIA BEDUIN 68, 69

The Jebelia are one of the most interesting of the Sinai Beduin tribes. They live in the neighbourhood of Jebel Katherina. Although they dress like Beduin and speak Arabic, their physiognomy is different from that of other Beduin tribes. They are said, plausibly enough, to be descended from Wallachian and Egyptian slaves settled here by Justinian in the 6th century to guard the monastery and act as servants to the monks. There are also Jebelia in Wadi Feiran. A closely related tribe, the Moatara, live in the neighbourhood of Tor, where they are acknowledged as experts in date-palm cultivation. Both Jebelia and Moatara work in the monastery gardens and look after the monastery's property. The Jebelia were formerly Christians but were subsequently converted to Islam. The other Beduin tribes despise the Jebelia, whom they call peasants or slaves, and do not intermarry with them.

Plate 53

A fairly good road leads westward from it to the high granite region of Jebel Musa, whence it continues through Wadi Feiran and the copper and turquoise mining districts to the Suez coast. We travelled along this road in commando cars and Jeeps, but were unable to stop for any length of time. We saw many buildings by the roadside, as well as Nabataean rock inscriptions, testifying that this was a main route for travellers then, too.

At Dhahab this road joins the coast road that runs down from Eilat to Sherm el Sheikh. From the port of Dhahab ships certainly sailed to the coast of Arabia. Almost opposite Dhahab is the small town of Maqna, which became well known thanks to its strong Jewish settlement at the beginning of the Mohammedan era.

We failed to find any pre-Nabataean remains in Dhahab, but we can be sure that the highways had remained the same throughout the various periods and that Dhahab had been an important junction even before the Nabataeans.

The identification of Dhahab and Dizahab is not impossible, though we were unable to find any direct support for it. However, even if the identification is certain, we must remember that Dizahab is mentioned only at the beginning of the Book of Deuteronomy, which is relatively late, in a general description of the region in which the events of the Exodus took place; it does not figure in the list of stations of Num. xxxiii.

The most important addition to our knowledge of any one of these stations was made by us, ironically enough, in the course of a more or less subsidiary investigation relating to a different period entirely. We were able to throw new light on the identification of the Byzantine site of Jotabe.[1]

The name occurs frequently in Byzantine sources as that of an island in the Gulf of Eilat (Aqaba) of great importance, in view of its dominance of the sea traffic to Eilat.

In the fifth and sixth centuries of the present era the island changed hands a number of times. It was conquered by a Persian named Ammorcessus, who drove the Byzantine customs men off the island. It is possible that a Jewish merchant settlement took root on the island at this time. At the end of the fifth century the Romans regained occupation but probably left the Jewish settlement undisturbed in its rights. So much we may learn from Procopius, who relates that the Emperor Justinian put an end to the island's autonomy (c. 535 A.D.) and brought it under Roman rule. Thenceforth it was the see of a bishop, whose name figures among those of Southern Palestinian bishops who participated in Church Councils in the sixth century.

The Jewish historian Graetz obviously exaggerated when he described this as a 'Jewish kingdom'. Nevertheless, this Jewish settlement in the Gulf of Eilat was by no means insignificant. There was also an important Jewish community in Maqna, on the eastern shore of the Gulf. We read that with the rise of Mohammed these Jews, together with all the others in the region, went to settle in Eilat to escape the Prophet's armies. Mohammed, however, hastened to enter into a treaty of friendship with them and persuaded them to return to their town. This free, militant Jewish settlement in the region of the Gulf of Eilat answers well to what we know of the Jews who for a short time dominated the commerce of Eilat from their island base of Jotabe. These Jews were there living on the edge of the Roman empire and had very largely succeeded in freeing themselves from the Byzantine yoke.

Jotabe is usually identified with the island of Tiran. More than any other this

[1] cf. Rothenberg's investigation of the island of Fara'un, pp. 86-92, 112 (40, 43) and Hashimshoni, pp. 185-189.

island is fitted for the role of naval base guarding the approach to Eilat, for it   Plate 38
dominates the narrow straits at the southern tip of the Gulf of Eilat. Between the
island of Tiran and Ras Nusrani, which lies opposite it on the coast (north of Sherm
el Sheikh) are a number of reefs which leave only two narrow, deep passages for
shipping. Navigation in this part of the Gulf is extremely dangerous; the wrecks of
two ships that ended up on the reefs of Tiran can still be seen. It is no coincidence
that the Egyptians set up their batteries here in order to prevent Israeli shipping
passing through the straits. The identification of Jotabe with Tiran seems to be
fully borne out by Procopius, who says that Jotabe was more than a thousand stadia
distant from Eilat, i.e. about 130 miles, roughly the length of the Gulf coast. Procopius goes on to say that after negotiating the straits one reaches the open sea
and is no longer able to see the mainland on the right. All this seems to add up to
the certainty of the Jotabe–Tiran identification.

We hoped to find remains of the settlement on the island. It was out of the
question, indeed, that a settlement of this kind, lasting for a comparatively long
period, should not have left behind it recognizable remains, e.g., harbour, fortress,
living quarters, synagogue and, of course, a church. To our astonishment, after
intensive search, we found nothing at all!

On my first visit to the island I stayed there a few hours. It is not as small as it
seems at first sight, being about nine miles in length and five in breadth. In the
south there are mountain ranges rising to a height of more than 1,600 feet. The
utter desolation of the island took me completely by surprise: no water, no vegetation, no remains of any settlement or traces of any husbandry—it had been a wilderness from the earliest times! I climbed to the top of one of the hills and surveyed
the scene through my field glasses: nothing, absolutely nothing that might even
hint at settlement or life of any kind. Perhaps traces of settlement might lie buried
somewhere in the recesses of the mountains?

Afterwards some colleagues roamed around the island, particularly Shmarya
Gutman, who spent more than a week exploring it. I myself returned to the island
after a short interval, together with the members of Professor Mazar's archaeological
expedition. Shmarya led us to his 'finds': some heaps of stones with flint implements
nearby denoting an early settlement of a temporary nature; and, on the northern
shore, on the beach itself, a few heaps of stones and some shells, with a number of
Roman-Byzantine sherds—doubtless remains left by fishermen who had found
temporary shelter here. This, evidently, was the sum total of the life existing on this
desolate island through all the course of its history. Even discounting Graetz's
'Jewish kingdom', these meagre heaps could not have accounted, even for the
existence of the humblest autonomous settlement or community of Byzantine
merchants and customs collectors.

We are forced to conclude, therefore, that the identification of Jotabe with the
island of Tiran is mistaken. Where, then, *is* Jotabe?

The only other island that could have any real claim to be the ancient Jotabe
is the small island of Fara'un, 10 miles south-east of Eilat, off the western coast of   Plate 40
the Gulf. It lies off the south-eastern tip of the bay of Taba, from which it is separated
by a narrow channel about 200 yards wide. It is a small island, about 300 yards
long, with ancient fortresses on rising ground at each end of it. There is a small
harbour, with good natural protection, in the middle of the island, facing the
mainland to the west. Most of the visible remains are of the Mameluke period,
but here and there it is possible to trace beneath these the remains of a fortress

dating from the Crusades. Along the shore of the island remains of a wall, probably more ancient, can be detected. On a small island such as this, covered with remains of late building, it is of course difficult to find early sherds, and on our short visit we were unable to find any that we could assign to a period earlier than the Crusades. However, Beno Rothenberg collected a few sherds which were clearly Byzantine and Professor Glueck, too, states that the earliest remains he succeeded in discovering on the island were Byzantine.

The sailors who established themselves on the island were able to control the maritime traffic to Aqaba, only 10 miles to the north. The strategic importance of the island, lying in a key position close to the mainland as it does, has also been utilized in recent times. We have to admit that Fara'un does not tally with the description of Jotabe given by Procopius, who probably placed it wrongly at the southern end of the Gulf, but the complete absence of any remains at all on the island of Tiran means that we are unable to confirm Procopius's identification in any case.

At this stage it will be opportune to consider whether perhaps the Byzantine Jotabe is not to be identified with the Biblical *Jotbathah*, which is mentioned as the station-but-one before Ezion-gaber in the itinerary of the Exodus: 'And they removed from Jotbathah, and encamped at Ebronah. And they departed from Ebronah, and encamped at Ezion-gaber' (Num. xxxiii. 34–35). As long as the site of the Byzantine Jotabe was sought at a remote distance from Eilat there could obviously be no question of connecting it with the Biblical Jotbathah.

As soon as the archaeological facts force us to look for Jotabe elsewhere, however, and the island of Fara'un is seen to be its most probable site, the question arises whether both Jotabe and Jotbathah may not be identifiable with Taba, 6 miles south of Eilat, at present just outside Israel's borders. The name Taba is very reminiscent of Jotbathah, of course, and the fact that the Biblical name has been preserved during the Byzantine period in a region—not far from Eilat— where the Biblical sources would lead us to expect to find the Biblical site, strengthen the case for the identification of the two places.

The recent trend has been to identify Jotbathah with Ain Ghadian, 25 miles north of Eilat, in the Araba. Four reasons are given:

I. Jotbathah appears to have been one of the main halting-places on the itinerary, and one of the most fertile, being described in Deut. x. 7 as 'a land of rivers of waters'. This must be taken as highly relative, of course, bearing in mind the usual meagre water supply in the desert; but the fact is that Ain Ghadian has one of the best springs in the Araba.

II. Numerous archaeological remains have been found at Ain Ghadian, dating from both the period of the First Temple and the Roman-Byzantine period.

III. The Arabs call the salt marsh south of the spring *Sabkh et Taba*, which perhaps preserves the Biblical name.

IV. On the road from Ain Ghadian to Eilat there is another scanty spring, Ain Defiyeh, which can perhaps be identified with the Biblical Ebronah, which is on the road to Ezion-gaber.

If we accept this identification then we must abandon the attempt to connect the Biblical Jotbathah with the Byzantine Jotabe, as obviously a spot 25 miles north of Eilat cannot be linked with an island in the heart of the Gulf.

But all the reasons listed above in favour of Ain Ghadian apply with equal force to Taba. Moreover, it must be borne in mind that the verbal similarity applies to the names of the oasis and its spring themselves, and not to a geographical feature in their vicinity.

We were able to pay a rather hurried visit to Taba, by which we were greatly impressed. It is quite a luxuriant desert oasis, on the shore of the Gulf, into which roads lead from the east. We saw many wells, indicating that it is not necessary to dig more than a few feet to reach water. In ancient times the settlement of Taba was obviously more important than that of Ain Ghadian, for both in Taba itself and in its satellite Tuweiba ('little Taba'), a mile or two south, we came across dozens of early structures, partly covered with sand and dust. Admittedly we were able to obtain only a few sherds, mostly Roman, but there can be no question but that Taba was an important oasis even in pre-Roman times. Of great interest, too, are the rock drawings and numerous inscriptions at the wadi entrances, testifying that here was an important trade route in the Nabataean period. The name of the place, its abundant water supply and its early remains make Taba not less suitable than Ain Ghadian for identification with Jotbathah, nor does its distance from Eilat favour such an identification less than does Ain Ghadian's. The ancient seaport of Eilat (the Biblical Elath) lay on the north-eastern tip of the Gulf of Aqaba, near the present-day port of Aqaba. Ezion-gaber, it is true, lay in the centre of the gulf-head, but Nelson Glueck's excavations showed that it had not been built until Solomon's time; hence Num. xxxiii. 35, 36 can refer only to Elath—known at the time of the monarchy as Ezion-gaber—lying further east. Near modern Eilat, too—which the Arabs call Umm Rashrash—remains of a temporary settlement have been found, and if we adopt the identification Jotbathah-Taba no difficulty arises in identifying Ebronah with Umm Rashrash or its environs.

In the writer's view, the identification of the Byzantine Jotabe with Jeziret Fara'un tips the balance in favour of the identification of Jotbathah with Taba. Moreover, locating the Biblical Jotbathah *south* of Eilat gives us a strong indication, for the first time, that in the course of their wanderings the Israelites moved southwards in the Peninsula, too. There is an echo of a tradition to this effect in the Pentateuch. The first chapter of Deuteronomy emphasizes the long distance between the mountain of God and Kadesh-barnea: 'And when we departed from Horeb, we went through all that great and terrible wilderness . . . and we came to Kadesh-barnea' (Deut. i. 19). We have an even clearer pointer at the very beginning of the chapter: 'There are *eleven days' journey* from Horeb by the way of Mount Seir to Kadesh-barnea' (Deut. i. 2). Eleven days does in fact correspond roughly to the time needed for the journey from Kadesh-barnea to the region of Jebel Musa, along the direct road south that hugs the coast of the Gulf of Aqaba. We know, for example, that a monk named Ammonius visited St Catherine's *c.* 373. The journey from Jerusalem to the traditional Mountain of God took him eighteen days. From Jerusalem to Kadesh is roughly a third of the whole distance, so he must have taken 10–12 days from Kadesh to the monastery.

Now, however, we are confronted with a further difficulty. What is the reason for the different names under which the mountain of God appears in the Bible? In the verses we have just quoted, for instance, it appears as Horeb, not Sinai. Horeb occurs more often in Deuteronomy, but is found in Exodus, too (iii. 1; xvii. 6; xxxiii. 6).

Are Horeb and Sinai interchangeable names for one and the same mountain, as Seir and Edom are interchangeable names for the same territory? Or is one of the names that of a range of mountains and the other the name of a specific peak

Plate 48

in it, as Hermon is a peak in the Sirion range, and Tabor in the Galilean range? Or have we here two different traditions about two different mountains, which in the course of time merged into one?

At present the data that would enable us to give a confident answer to these questions are lacking. Clearly Mount Horeb lay in the south and was already identified with Mount Sinai in Bible times. It was certainly to this region that Elijah came after going 'forty days and forty nights unto Horeb the mount of God' (I Kings xix. 8).

Is it possible to assume that the sacred and ancient mountain of Sinai lay in fact in the region of Kadesh-barnea, although in the period of the monarchy it was identified with Mount Horeb in the south of Sinai? Our discoveries in the region of Kadesh-barnea make it difficult to accept such an assumption. It is not merely that Kadesh lay in the border country of Canaan and Judah; it is now clear that the whole region came under Israelite control.

Fig. 4 From the beginning of the monarchy a strong line of defences, based on a network of fortresses and watchtowers, had been maintained here. Apart from the strong fortress guarding Ain el Qudeirat we now know that there were forts placed at strategic points along the roads leading to Kadesh. It is clear that the kings of Israel and Judah attached great importance to obtaining complete control of the region and of its important lines of communication. Kadesh-barnea was an integral part of the kingdom of Judah, and would certainly be easily accessible. Nor have we any reason to doubt the etymological evidence (Heb. *Kadesh*, 'holy'), and if the writer's conclusion about the wall is correct, the tradition of holiness receives additional confirmation. By no stretch of imagination, then, could Kadesh be considered a far-off, little-known region, inaccessible to the Israelites of the monarchy. How can we possibly assume, this being the case, that the site of the sacred mountain of Sinai, so indelibly engraved in the nation's mind, could be so quickly forgotten, if it lay in Kadesh-barnea? Although we cannot affirm positively that Mount Horeb and Mount Sinai were originally one and the same mountain, we can be reasonably sure that both of them were far distant from any centre of population and inaccessible to the Israelites of the monarchy. All the evidence leads us inevitably southwards, to the mountain ranges of southern Sinai.

To the names Sinai and Horeb we can add a third, *Mount Paran*, which appears in poetical passages in the Bible. In the blessing of Moses we read: 'The Lord came from Sinai, and rose up from Seir unto them; he shined forth from *mount Paran*, and he came with ten thousand of saints' (Deut. xxxiii. 2). Similarly in Habakkuk, iii. 3: 'God came from Teman, and the Holy One from *mount Paran*.' It seems likely that in the verses the sacred mountain of Sinai-Horeb is given a more general name, Mount Paran, linked with the wilderness of Paran. The Mountain of God changed names as frequently as did the deserts of the south. If we could locate the wilderness of Paran, would it help us to identify Mount Sinai?

The specific statement in Num. x. 12 precludes our equating Sinai and Paran ('And the children of Israel took their journeys *out of the wilderness of Sinai*; and the cloud rested *in the wilderness of Paran*'). Taberah, Kibroth-hattaavah and Hazeroth lay in the wilderness of Paran (Num. xi–xii), but as we are unable to identify them they do not help us to locate Paran. Hazeroth, indeed, could possibly be identified with Ain Hasera, north on the road from Jebel Musa, but we cannot reach any firm conclusions from one solitary place-name. The most precise *point d'appui* are Kadesh-barnea and Elath. Kadesh-barnea is specifically mentioned in the story of the sending of the spies: 'And they went . . . unto the wilderness of Paran, to Kadesh' (Num. xiii. 26). The last place reached by the four kings of the north in their battles against the kings of the plain is 'El-paran which is by the wilderness' (Gen. xiv. 6), whither they came from Mount Seir after moving down the plateau of trans-Jordan. From here they turned, 'And they returned and came to En-mishpat, which is Kadesh (-barnea)'. We may reasonably assume, therefore, that the reference is to Elath, on the border of the wilderness of Paran; hence its designation El(ath)-paran. This tends to support the view that the wilderness of Paran corresponds to Et Tih ('the wanderers' desert') or even only the northern part of this vast desert plateau in the north of the Sinai peninsula. The fact that elsewhere the Bible describes Kadesh-barnea as being in the wilderness of Zin (Num. xx. i; xxvii. 14), is accounted for by its location on the borders of both deserts and hence its possible inclusion in the territory of either.

However, an extremely important archaeological discovery made during the last survey of Sinai now compels us to re-examine all our previous assumptions. An expedition headed by Professor Mazar examined the tell of the desert oasis of Feiran. This is the principal oasis, stretching for a few miles, of southern Sinai. It lies at the foot of the lofty Mount Serbal and is fed by the melting snow that covers the summits of the high granite mountains in winter. A purling stream provides water for graceful date-palms, orchards and flourishing vegetable-gardens. Rising prominently in the middle of the oasis is a tell on top of which many interesting remains of a large monastery of the Byzantine period have been preserved, and scattered all about the tell, over an area of about ten acres, the remains of buildings and walls are discernible. A careful examination by the Mazar expedition of the sherds they collected revealed that, apart from numerous Roman-Byzantine and early Arab sherds, the site abounded in Nabataean sherds. In addition, the site produced sherds of the Hellenistic period, Persian sherds and some wheel-burnished sherds typical of the kingdom of Judah, belonging to Iron Age II, i.e., the period of the kings of Judah during the time of the First Temple. This, then, is the only tell discovered so far in Sinai—perhaps the only tell there at all—displaying a fairly prolonged continuity of settlement: at the very least, from the Iron Age, c. 9th–8th centuries B.C., through the Persian-Hellenistic and Roman-Byzantine periods up to the early Arab period.

Plate 55

Feiran lies on the road running from the Gulf of Suez to the Jebel Musa region. As we have already noted, from here the road continues to Dhahab, on the coast of the Gulf of Eilat (Aqaba). Scores of Sinaitic inscriptions, mostly Nabataean, but some Greek and Arabic, written on the rocks by merchants passing in their caravans, have been found in Wadi Feiran itself and in other wadis nearby. Particularly in Wadi Mukattab—the Arab name means 'Valley of the Inscriptions'—hundreds of rock inscriptions and drawings stare the spectator in the face. These roads teemed with life in the Nabataean period, as the inscriptions testify; they linked the coasts of the two gulfs, and thereby Egypt and southern Arabia. Feiran, lying on the chief waterspring along this route, dominates these roads, as it doubtless did throughout the period of settlement in the area.

Fig. 1

Here, too, are Sinai's ancient copper and turquoise mines. Ancient mines have also been discovered in the neighbourhood of Jebel Musa and also to the east of it. On our last expedition we found a concentration of copper slag in Dhahab, proving either that there were ancient mines here, too, or that the ore had been brought hither by the merchant caravans. Mention has already been made of the Egyptian temple built in the centre of the ancient mining area in Serabit el Khadem, east of the modern manganese enterprise in Abu Zenima. From here the road, again dotted with rock inscriptions along the whole length, leads directly south-east towards Jebel Musa. This road passes alongside Wadi el Sheikh, the upper arm of Wadi Feiran. The road to the coast from Feiran itself runs north-west, as mentioned, alongside Wadi Mukattab and Wadi Shellala. At the junction of the two wadis it turns to the foot of Jebel Maghara, the 'mountain of the caves'. This is one of the chief of the ancient Egyptian mining centres, in which numerous hieroglyphic rock inscriptions have been found. The road joins the coast at Ain Markha, situated at the southern end of a pleasant bay, south of Abu Zenima. Near the coast here

Plate 34

Professor Albright's expedition found, in 1947, an ancient Egyptian port, dating, according to the sherds, from the 15th–13th centuries B.C.; that is to say, the port was probably in existence at the time of the Exodus. On our own expeditions we found the additional remains of a second fortress, a little south and nearer the coast. Unfortunately it was covered with sand, and we were unable to find any sherds by which we could ascertain its date. Here, in the bay of Markha, were the post and the transit station for the caravans that came from Egypt by land and sea, and from here they went to the mountains of the mines and continued by the caravan routes to the Gulf of Aqaba in the east. *Markha* in the west and *Dhahab* in the east were the two road-heads on the coasts, and *Feiran* in between was the chief area of settlements—perhaps the only one—that existed in the region in ancient times. To round off our topographical survey, we shall mention only that Jebel Musa looks down on the Markha–Dhahab road.

Plate 55

Surprisingly enough, this tell, now known as Feiran, at an earlier stage in its history bore the name of *Paran*, identical with the Biblical name. In the Byzantine period it was an important city, frequently mentioned in the sources, with its own cathedral and bishop. The Roman geographer Ptolemaeus, who lived in the first half of the second century A.D., mentions Paran in his *Geography* as being situated here. Hence it is clear that the name preceded the advent of Christianity and could not have been introduced by Christian monks. Archaeological investigation, as we have already said, has now shown that the settlement of Feiran existed without any significant gap in continuity from the time of the Judaean kings to that of Ptolemaeus. It is difficult to see any reason why the name of the settlement should have changed in this period. It is unlikely that Paran was a new name given to the site in the Hellenistic-Roman period, though it sometimes happened that sites were renamed in this period, without, however, being able in the majority of cases to preserve the new name for any great length of time. No, it is clear that Paran is an ancient Semitic-Biblical name belonging to the wilderness of the South.

We can now assert, then, with considerable confidence that our tell was called *Paran* as far back as the reign of the Judaean kings and that it was without any doubt the chief centre of settlement in the whole of southern Sinai. In other words it was the capital of the Sinai peninsula both in Biblical and post-Biblical times.

In the light of this fresh evidence can we continue to adhere to the hitherto accepted view that the Biblical 'Paran' and 'Wilderness of Paran' do not refer to the region we have been discussing, but can be located only in northern Sinai?

I venture to suggest another possibility, based on the ancient sources and supported by the Bible: *Paran, not Sinai, was the original name by which the whole of the Sinai peninsula was known in Biblical times.* The wilderness of Paran was not confined to the desert of Et Tih or its northern part, but was the ancient name for the whole of the vast triangle which we now call the wilderness of Sinai or the Sinai peninsula.

Let us test this thesis by reference to the various verses in which Paran is mentioned in the Bible. The fact that in poetical passages Paran occurs instead of Mount Sinai or Mount Horeb now becomes susceptible of a perfectly simple explanation if we assume that the wilderness of Sinai was merely a specific part of a greater wilderness of Paran. Such an assumption would also explain why Kadesh-barnea is sometimes stated to be in the wilderness of Zin, for the wilderness of Zin is simply the northern part of the wilderness of Paran.

In Gen. xiv. 6 'El(ath)-paran, which is by the wilderness' shows, of course, that the wilderness of Paran, stretching south, started from Elath, but it is also interesting to note that Paran is used here as an attribute of place; cf. Bethlehem-*Judah*, or Mizpeh-*Gilead*.

At the beginning of Deuteronomy, Paran—not Sinai—is mentioned as one of the places where 'Moses spoke unto all Israel on this side Jordan in the wilderness, in the plain over against the Reed Sea, between *Paran*, and Tophel, and Laban, and Hazeroth, and Dizahab' (Deut. i. 1). Incidentally, Paran is mentioned here between the names of various *places* in the South.

Occasionally *Paran* appears as a general name for the desert south of Canaan. For example, when Hagar and Ishmael flee from the wilderness of Beersheba: 'And he dwelt in the wilderness of *Paran*: and his mother took him a wife out of the land of Egypt' (Gen. xxi. 21); when Haddad the Edomite flees from David 'and they arose out of Midian, and came to *Paran*, and they took men with them out of *Paran*, and they came to Egypt, unto Pharaoh king of Egypt' (I Kings xi. 18). When David fled from Saul (I Sam. xxv. 1), he 'went down to the wilderness of *Paran*' (the Septuagint, it is true, has 'wilderness of Maon').

Per contra, Sinai, *wilderness of Sinai* occur in the Bible only in connexion with the Revelation at Mount Sinai and in the accounts of the Israelites' wanderings in the desert. Unlike Paran, Sinai is never once mentioned incidentally, in a context not related to the Relevation or to the Exodus. Nor is any place, apart from Mount Sinai itself, ever mentioned as lying within the wilderness of Sinai: 'For they were departed from Rephidim, and were come to the desert of Sinai, and had pitched in the wilderness; and there Israel camped before the mount' (Exod. xix. 2).

There is only one verse which seems to refute this thesis: 'And the children of Israel took their journeys out of the wilderness of Sinai, and the cloud rested in the wilderness of Paran' (Num. x. 12). Does not this prove that the wilderness of Sinai is not included in the wilderness of Paran?

Even if we assume that it is not, we must admit that after the Israelites had left Mount Sinai, they came immediately to the wilderness of Paran. So that even in this case the wilderness of Sinai would not comprise a large region; it would extend only, in fact, to the area around the sacred mountain of Sinai, and it would have no oasis, for the children of Israel camped in the *wilderness*.

However, Num. x. 12 cannot really be held to disprove our theory, as the subsequent account shows. From Mount Sinai the children of Israel move to the wilderness of Paran; after three days' journey they reach Taberah, from thence they go on to Kibbroth-Hattaavah and Hazeroth (Num. xi-xii), evidently all places in the wilderness of Paran. Later we read: 'And afterward the people removed from Hazeroth, and pitched in the wilderness of Paran' (Num. xii. 16). If we argue from Num. x. 12 that Mount Sinai must have been outside the wilderness of Paran, then equally we must argue from Num. xii. 16 that Hazeroth was outside the wilderness of Paran, but Num. xi. 35 clearly indicates the contrary. When the Israelites move from one specific resting-place they find themselves once more in the great wilderness of Paran; we cannot infer that because a place is named immediately before the wilderness of Paran it is thereby excluded from the geographical area of Paran. And the very fact that the mountain of God is called Mount Paran proves that it came within the geographical confines of the wilderness of Paran.

An indirect confirmation of our thesis is provided in the long list of stations given in Num. xxxiii: 'And they removed from the Reed Sea, and encamped in the *wilderness of Sin* . . . *wilderness of Sinai* . . . And they removed from Ezion-gaber, and pitched in the *wilderness of Zin*, which is Kadesh . . .'. All the great desert regions are listed in this catalogue of place-names *except* the wilderness of Paran, although precisely this wilderness is frequently mentioned elsewhere in Numbers. Why? Surely because the wilderness of Paran was the general term for the whole of the territory in which the various stations of the Exodus lay, and there would have been no point in mentioning it in connexion with a list of particular places.

To sum up: an analysis of the Biblical sources shows that they are in no way incompatible with the location of Paran in the south of the Sinai peninsula. More, everything indicates that the name Paran had a much more general significance and referred to a much larger region than the other regional names. It seems to me, therefore, particularly in view of the recent archaeological discoveries on the spot, that we are no longer justified in rejecting the identification of Feiran with the Biblical Paran. It seems likely that this particular spot called Paran gave its name to the whole wilderness; it may well be, also, that it had another name linked with 'Paran', as in El-paran, and that in the course of time this special name was forgotten and only the second part of the name was preserved.

The identification of Feiran with the Biblical Paran affords decisive support, of course, for the contention that the Mountain of God, Mount Sinai-Horeb-Paran, must be sought in one of the majestic granite peaks of this region. These lofty pinnacles that rise far off in the depths of the wilderness strike awe and reverence into the heart of every beholder. In this region travel-weary wanderers would find a safe refuge in the oases tucked away among the deep river-beds. Flanking these oases were the ancient copper and turquoise mines at the entrances to which the Egyptians had left their boastful inscriptions more than a thousand years before the Exodus. In these mines worked Semitic slaves, perhaps related to the Kenites, who inscribed here the first alphabetical writings. Here they worshipped the mighty goddess called 'Baalath' in the Proto-Sinaitic inscriptions.

We know to-day that the Israelites did not intend to make their way here when they left Egypt, but that they made straight for Kadesh-barnea on their way to Canaan, and that Kadesh-barnea remained their chief centre through all the years of their wandering. But if the Israelites wandered in the wilderness for a whole generation, which no one doubts, is it conceivable that they always formed *one compact group* in their peregrinations and in their encampments? Even if their number had not exceeded a few thousand, equivalent to the present Beduin population of the Sinai desert, there was not a single spot which could have supported them more than a few days, not even Ain el Qudeirat, the richest of the oases in northern Sinai.

Plate 11

The Israelites' initial destination was Kadesh-barnea, along the route between Canaan and Egypt that the Patriarchs of the nation had taken before them. But when their first attempt to penetrate Canaan was frustrated by the stiff resistance they met from the king of Arad, 'which dwelt in the south (Negeb)', they were forced to wander in the wilderness for a whole generation and to abide in, among other places, Kadesh-barnea for 'many days'. We must assume that at this period there began a dispersal of the tribes, clans, households. This was necessary if they were to eke out a bare subsistence in the vast desert by finding pasturage for their sheep or by seasonal tilling of the soil or by trading with the passing caravans or by brigandage. There is no reason to assume that they massed together in the northern part of the desert without branching off along the western shore of the Gulf of Eilat (Aqaba) down to the south of the Peninsula, to the region of the ancient copper and turquoise mines. This did not preclude their concentrating periodically round specially hallowed spots, just as, after they had entered Canaan, they had special holy places round which they concentrated in that country, for example Gilgal, Shechem, Shiloh and such mountains as Tabor and Carmel.

The major difficulties encountered in plotting the itinerary of the Exodus disappear as soon as we abandon the theory of all the twelve tribes moving in a single compact group all through the years of wandering. The opposing theory of dispersion is hardly contradicted by the tradition of movement from one halting-place to another, from one oasis to another. Without any doubt the households, the tribes, moved according to season from one water-source to another. Only on specific occasions did they gather together for a popular assembly and for great popular festivals. Hence it is quite possible that in their wanderings the Israelites reached the southern part of the Sinai peninsula and that here they witnessed the supreme moment of the Revelation which was to leave its impress on them and on succeeding generations.

Obviously we cannot identify Mount Horeb (Sinai?) itself. Since Byzantine times the title has been traditionally assigned to Jebel Musa, a peak rising in lofty grandeur to over 6,500 feet in the southern mountain ranges. But facing it Jebel Katherina rises to nearly 9,000 feet, and from its summit Jebel Musa seems merely one of a number of lesser heights. The tradition of the holiness of Jebel Kathcrina may be related to the ancient worship of Hathor-Baalath. Nabataean inscriptions show that the mountain was a centre of pilgrimage in pre-Byzantine times.

Plate 53

Jebel Serbal is lower than each of these mountains, but it stands apart from the others in solitary grandeur, the most imposing peak in the whole chain. It looks straight down on the largest of the oases in southern Sinai, Feiran-Paran, and the dramatic contrast between the luxuriant plain and the bare mountain is tremendously impressive. Its name has a touch of antiquity about it, too; it may be a corruption of Sur (Heb. 'rock of')-Baal.

Plate 57

However, though we are unable to identify Mount Sinai with complete accuracy, we can now confidently assert that as far back as the United Monarchy it was identified with Mount Horeb in the south of the Peninsula. We have no means of telling whether this identification was correct; on the other hand, we have no evidence which would enable us to challenge it.

Summing up, recent research has strengthened the case for locating Mount Sinai in the south of the Peninsula, with the *caveat*, however, that the Israelite journeyings in the wilderness must not be regarded as a planned itinerary adhered to at all times by a single group, but that in the Biblical story the strands of the different directions taken by different groups of the 'desert generation' at different times were woven into a single whole.

THE VALLEY OF THE INSCRIPTIONS

At Ras el Nagb, the peak north-west of Eilat on the Sinai-Israel border, the 'Pilgrim's Way' (Darb el Haj) enters Israel territory. The Darb el Haj starts near Suez, continues by way of the Mitla Pass, Qal'at el Nakhl and Themed and then descends in hairpin bends from Ras el Nagb to the Gulf of Eilat (Aqaba), whence it enters Saudi Arabia and terminates at Mecca.

In ancient times three main roads cut across the Peninsula. The southernmost one, the 'Way of Mount Seir' probably followed the same path as the Pilgrim's Way, and extended to Ezion-geber-Eilat. Near Eilat, however, the Darb el Haj, which was built by the Mameluke Sultans, parted company from the ancient 'Way of Mount Seir'. The latter, instead of passing through Ras el Nagb wound its way southward through steep, narrow wadis to a point near Taba. Thence it continued along the coast.

In the time of the Second Temple and during the ensuing centuries this road became an important caravan route for Nabataean merchants who were wont to immortalize themselves by leaving inscriptions on every suitable rock surface that came to hand. They were not alone in doing so, and hence there are to be found along the southern roads of Sinai and in the wadis near Taba, not far from Eilat, Nabataean, Greek, Latin and Arabic inscriptions, consisting chiefly of the names of travellers who passed by here in distant ages. These inscriptions are particularly plentiful at the ancient staging-points along the road.

During the brief occupation of Sinai by Israeli forces, young geologists discovered a canyon whose massive, hollowed-out walls and kalaedoscopic range of colouring were of extraordinary beauty. This canyon was subsequently investigated by Dan Gilead, a young member of the settlement of Beer Ora in the Araba. He was surprised to find amongst other inscriptions a seven-branched candelabrum with an adjacent ram's horn—ancient Jewish emblems—drawn on the walls of the canyon. He realized at once the importance of his discovery and sent for scholars to study the inscriptions on the spot. Decipherment revealed many highly interesting inscriptions, the most important of which is a Jewish-Aramaic inscription in Nabataean characters giving the name of the great seaport of Maqna on the eastern shore of the Gulf of Eilat (Aqaba) and the name of a Jewish traveller who lived on the island of Jotabe.

70 QA EL NAGB

Beyond the heights of Ras el Nagb, immediately after the point where the Darb el Haj forks from the Gaza Road, stretches the dun-coloured, completely flat and completely desolate plain of Qa el Nagb. Its sole features are a few large circles of boulders. The plain, which extends for about a mile, is bordered by a range of dark, rugged hills.

71 THE CANYON OF WADI UMM SIDEIRA

The photograph shows the entrance to the canyon. The first inscription (shown in Plate 83) encountered by the traveller is on the right-hand wall, about ten feet above ground level.

A DRY WATERFALL IN WADI UMM SIDEIRA 72

For about 200 yards movement in the canyon is possible, though difficult. After that, further progress is blocked by this huge dry waterfall, over 200 feet deep. The photograph gives some idea of the many-hued rock of which the mountains in this area are composed.

GENERAL VIEW OF WADI UMM SIDEIRA 73

This wadi is one of the northern branches of Wadi Taba. Its banks are of red, grey and yellowish Nubian sandstone. Starting as a series of flat gullies, it becomes a deep gorge about half-a-mile north of a range of lofty peaks, and a few hundred yards farther on it narrows into a canyon. On the walls, about 25 to 50 feet high, of this canyon were found many rock drawings the existence of which had not previously been known.

NABATAEAN INSCRIPTION IN WADI UMM SIDEIRA 74

This reads: 'Peace peace peace peace. [May he give you] your reward. Ben Abu'. (B. Sapir).

DRAWING OF JEWISH CANDELABRUM 75

Immediately opposite the drawing of the candelabrum and ram's horn (Plates 77, 85), Beno Rothenberg found another, much fainter, drawing of a candelabrum.

GREEK INSCRIPTION IN WADI UMM SIDEIRA 76

This is a close-up of the inscription to be seen in Plate 78. It reads 'The tomb of Basileus Kerdion the Thessalian'. (Professor A. Shalit).

ROCK DRAWING WITH JEWISH MOTIF AND GREEK AND 77 LATIN INSCRIPTIONS

Above the candelabrum (Menorah) in Wadi Umm Sideira the word AKRABOS is engraved in Greek characters. Left of the Menorah is engraved—probably later addition—VICTORÍA AUG [USTÍ] C [AESARÍS] in Latin.

71

72

74

75

76

ΑΚΡΑΒΟC

77

81

82

83

84

88

86

89

90

87

78 PART OF THE CANYON

The plate shows one side of the canyon where it opens out a little to form a small square. The inscription lower right is well protected from flood by the huge vaulting rock overhead. (See Plate 76).

79 NABATAEAN INSCRIPTION

The inscription reads: Peace to Candu the *Nawat* ('sailor'). (Dr A. Gargel and B. Sapir).

80 ALTAR (?)

At the entrance to the canyon is a rock embedded in the ground, suggesting an ancient 'altar'. The rock has a number of small indentations (cup-marks) and linear incisions. A number of drawings of ibex were found at this spot.

81 GREEK INSCRIPTION

This is difficult to read.

82 'AGRIPPAS' IN GREEK CHARACTERS

Apart from the word 'Agrippas' this inscription is difficult to decipher, as previous 'visitors' to the canyon have rubbed it over with charcoal.

83 GREEK INSCRIPTION AT THE HEAD OF THE CANYON

Engraved with a sharp stone on the wall of the canyon is a Greek inscription reading, in free translation: 'May Obolus ben Chanya (=Chananya?) be remembered for good fortune'. (Professor A. Shalit).

84 JEWISH-ARAMAIC INSCRIPTION IN NABATAEAN SCRIPT

This, the most interesting of the Wadi Umm Sideira inscriptions, was punched out with a sharp stone in a small square of the canyon, on the north-eastern wall. It reads: 'Akrabos son of Samuel of Maqna, of son-of-Sadia of Jotabe.' (B. Sapir).

85 CANDELABRUM, RAM'S HORN AND 'AKRABOS'
(detail of Plate 77)

On the north-east wall of the square in the canyon this engraving was found punched with a sharp stone, of a seven-branched candelabrum (Menorah) on a tripodal base, with to the left of it a ram's horn (Shofar) and to the right at faint representation, perhaps of a censer. On the opposite wall is another, fainter, engraving of a candelabrum, also seven-branched and on a three-pronged base. See Plate 75 and p. 85.

MONUMENT AT RAS EL NAGB COMMEMORATING 86
REPAIRING OF THE PILGRIM'S WAY [?]

Found by Beno Rothenberg by the wall of the police post at Ras el Nagb. The inscription reads: 'In the name of Allah the compassionate and the merciful this building was repaired in the name of the mighty, victorious Sultan Hasan and the mighty and victorious Sultan Mohammed Qal'aun on the 7th Rajab in the year 747 (=27th October 1346). (A. Ben Chorin).

TOMBSTONE IN SYRIAC AND GREEK CHARACTERS 87

This tombstone was found near Gaza by General Moshe Dayan. It has not been deciphered.

NABATAEAN SHERDS FROM THE NABATAEAN 88
SETTLEMENT IN WADI EL AIN

A Nabatacan settlement can be easily distinguished by its delicate painted pottery. Nabataean sherds have been found in the remotest parts of the Sinai peninsula.

MIDDLE BRONZE I SHERDS 89

These sherds are typical for the beginning of the Patriarchal period. They were discovered both in Palestine and in Sinai as far south as the sanctuary of Serabit el Khadem, where Beno Rothenberg discovered them within circles of stone surrounding the temple. Sherds taken from regions far apart exhibit nevertheless a remarkable similarity of material, form and decoration indicating great waves of Amorite invasion in the ancient East at this time. The two vertical lines of sherds on the left were collected at Ruweiset el Akheider; the two lines on the right come from Jebel el Ain.

IRON AGE (10TH–9TH CENTURIES B.C.) SHERDS FROM THE 90
FORTRESS OF AIN QADEIS

Sherds of hand-made pottery have been found near remains of the United Monarchy, from the 10th century B.C. onwards, throughout Sinai and particularly in the various regions of the Negeb. The discovery of this hand-made, as opposed to wheel-made pottery, caused considerable difficulties at first, but we know now that all over the Negeb and Sinai there was a long tradition of hand-made pottery down to the 6th–5th centuries B.C. The first sherd, on the left, in the second row shows the impress made by the mat on which the primitive pot was 'built'.

JEZIRET FARA'UN

AVIA HASHIMSHONI

PART SIX   JEZIRET FARA'UN

Jeziret Fara'un was partially surveyed by second-year students of the Haifa Technion as a practical exercise in scale-drawing.[1]

In the four days we spent on the island we measured the buildings on the northern hill and parts of the wall surrounding the ruins on both northern and southern hills. Unfortunately, difficulties arose as a result of which we were unable to complete the assignment we had set ourselves. In particular, we were unable to measure the area, marked H on our map, on which remains of dwellings were found. However, we were able to draw a general map of the island, to measure the height of the hills and to analyse the palace-like complex of buildings on the northern hill (C). In this paper we enumerate the various structures observed by us on the island and describe their architectural features.

Plate 40

The island known as Jeziret Fara'un or El Qureiye is a small, projecting island measuring some 325 yards from north to south, and, at its widest, some 160 yards from east to west. It lies approximately 10 miles south of Eilat, a little more than 300 yards from the western shore of the Gulf of Eilat (Aqaba).

There are three hillocks, A, B & C, running from north to south on the island. North, east and west (but not south) there is a flat strip of shore about 20 yards wide rising slightly above sea-level. To the west is a harbour and small port about 200 × 100 feet. The island is of granite throughout.

Of the three hills, the largest is the northern, C; it occupies about half the area of the island. Its flat table-top, measuring 330 × 80 feet, is 60 to 90 feet above sea-level. It is joined to the cone-shaped hill, A, (80 feet high), by an isthmus, B, a hundred yards or so in length. The island has no natural water-sources. There are cisterns cut in the rock on the island, but as the rainfall averages only some two inches per annum it is obvious that these cisterns were not used to collect rainwater, but to store water brought from the mainland, on which the island depended.

Geographically, the island's main features can be described briefly as its steep hills, its small port facing the mainland, and the narrow and comparatively calm strait separating it from the Sinai peninsula. It has strategic importance by virtue of its position at the junction of the Red Sea route to Southern Arabia and East Africa with the land routes to Syria and Egypt.

The hill-top walls make an impressive spectacle which tends to divert the casual visitor's attention from most of the equally interesting remains at ground-level. In the course of over four days' study of the island we were able to examine some of its less immediately striking features. On the first day we had the benefit of Beno Rothenberg's keen powers of observation.

[1] I should like to mention particularly the valuable assistance I received from David Shalev and Shimeon Tuchler, who contributed in no small measure to the success of the survey.

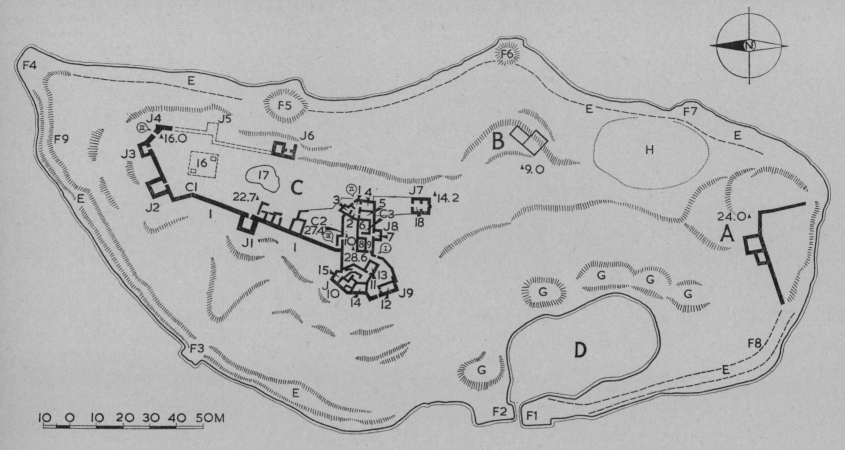

Fig. 16. Plan of Jeziret Fara'un (Avia Hashimshoni)

I propose an architectural classification of the various structures on the island into five groups; three at ground-level and two on the hill-tops.

At sea-level we distinguished:

1. a surrounding wall, E, with seven clear towers, F1 to F7, and two, F8 to F9, about which we were not certain.

2. ruins of vaulted buildings round the harbour.

3. a network of dwelling and street foundations occupying the area marked H. On the heights we distinguished:

4. several rooms and walls on hills A and B.

5. a citadel and palace crowning hill C.

Most of the structures on the island are built of dry, roughly-hewn granite. With material as hard as granite, particularly if only roughly dressed, mortar is unnecessary. We found the cross-bonding adequate. There are differences both in the type of construction and the quality of workmanship not only among the various structures, but in one and the same structure.

The most obvious differences occur in the tower, F3, in which the lower courses, of Cyclopean character, are succeeded by well-constructed middle courses, with a looser technique in the upper courses. Similar changes are exhibited in the masonry of the fortress, the northern part being accurately laid whereas the middle portions are looser. In the residential quarter there are differences between the workmanship of the keep-like room, 8, and the remainder of the complex. The structures on hills A and B have alternating high and low courses of stone, a type of construction which we know of in several other places, e.g., the Qasr Zuweira in the Judaean desert. A small quantity of limestone was used in the building of the palace.

Fig. 16

Plate 47

Plate 45

On the window jamb between rooms 4 and 5 Beno Rothenberg discovered an incised cross (Plate 44). The upper square corners of tower 7 are supported by '*pseudo stalactite*' limestone corbels; cisterns 13 and 16 are built mainly of limestone.

The cross led Beno Rothenberg to believe that the palace might have been a Crusader fortification in which room 8 was used as a dungeon and the lofty chamber 4 as a chapel. However, we have no means of telling when the stone with the cross, or any others, were laid. The changes in the quality of the workmanship do not necessarily point to different periods of construction, but could be accounted for by shortage of manpower or available stone or by the fact that in certain parts, e.g., the upper part of the walls, strength was essential.

The only indications of plastering appear in the palace section of the fortress. The roofs and intermediate floors were made of beaten earth (*terre pisée*) laid on a matting of palm-trunks. I am inclined to think that the buildings marked G were vaulted.

We observed that the foundation-remains of the wall surrounding the island, E, ran in two parallel lines, with intersecting ribs. This led Beno Rothenberg to assume that we were dealing with a casemate wall, but such an assumption would not account for the heaps of earth scattered about the foundation-remains, which suggest that the wall was double-skinned, filled with earth. Nevertheless, the possibility of a casemate wall, mainly in the area H, merits serious consideration.

Plate 43

Another interesting architectural detail is the bolt of gate III. It consists of a piece of wood eight inches square sliding horizontally into a cavity of similar dimensions. A similar system was used in El Meshella, as described by Domaszewski.[1]

Wall E, surrounding the island, runs along the shore-line up to the steep slope of hill A, where a thinner wall of possibly later date went up to the summit. The remains of this wall measure some 8 inches in width and 13 inches in height. The

Plate 45

best preserved tower, F3, measures 24 × 33 feet. It has a square base and slightly rounded corners at the top. The various towers on the island are spaced some 110 yards apart. The twin towers F1 and F2 guarded the entrance, still used by fishermen at high tide, to the harbour.

The foundation layers of the wall are embedded in hardened mortar, probably made of sand. Along the western shore we found a continuous low rampart. I believe this to be the inner filling of the wall which was left when the stones of the two skins were removed. Except for the towers, this wall is missing from the eastern shore, having probably been washed away by the waters of the Gulf. I am inclined to believe that a second harbour existed near tower F9 which was used to bring water from the mainland for storing in cistern 16. We estimated the wall would have taken some 30–40,000 work-days to build.

It is arguable that the wall was never finished, but I would suggest that the existence of the wall A is prima facie evidence that the whole wall was completed. In this case it would be obvious that the walls were at one time dismantled and only the filling of beaten earth left behind. Some of the stone from the wall was used for other building on the island, in spite of the fact that there was insufficient stone on the island for the outer surrounding wall. The lay-out of the buildings marked G suggests that there were probably warehouses around the small port.

The area H is of the greatest interest. The numerous dwellings which once existed here were razed to the ground, and the only remains consist of a network of upright stone blocks embedded in hardened mortar which resemble the foundation-remains of the surrounding wall. We found nothing which might afford a clue to

[1] R. E. Brünnow and A. Domaszewski, *Die Provincia Arabia* (Strassburg, 1902), vol. ii, p. 109.

the period when the structures here were built, nor to the use to which they were put, but the lay-out of the masonry is less haphazard than that of the better-preserved buildings on the island, and indicates a higher level of technical skill.

The remains on hills A and B were only cursorily examined by us. Those on the top of hill A are better preserved, with the roofs still intact. The bonding differs from the usual practice in that courses of normal width are separated by thin string courses.

We now come to the description of the remains on the top of hill C. The buildings and walls occupy the whole of the plateau-like summit. The external walls are built on the verge of the cliff and are accessible only from the north, where there is one gate, and from the south, where at one time there were two gates. The buildings comprise a fortified courtyard on the north and a residential complex on the south. Flanking the latter is a protruding structure containing a prayer niche to the south and a cluster of rooms, presumably the garrison's quarters, to the north.

Plate 47

The northern buildings are better constructed than the southern, and are probably older. The wall is adequately strengthened with towers spaced some 60–90 feet apart. Those to the west are fairly well preserved, and are two-storied. The towers on the east collapsed with portions of the wall as a result of their being built too near the edge of the cliff.

There are two pits in this area. That marked 17 is an open quarry; the other, 16, is a properly finished, vaulted cistern. The residential palace is situated above the other buildings (it is 93 feet above sea-level) and consists of two clusters of rooms (for men and women?). The western portion of the complex consists of several two-storied rooms (12, 14, 15 and presumably 17). Room 12, dubbed by us the Sultana's boudoir, commands a magnificent view. In the inner court, 13, there is a cistern with stairs leading to the bottom. The roof of the cistern is supported by twin arches, trimmed with red brickwood, radiating from a single column. The upper part of the arches looks modern.

In the eastern part of the palace the rooms of greatest interest are 8, a miniature keep, and 4, with its lofty window in which Beno Rothenberg found the incised cross.

Plate 44

There were three entrances to the palace. Access to the first, I, was gained by climbing the steep slope at the foot of the palace; the second, II, was reached by an easier gradient from hill B. There is no sign of a door which can be locked at entrance III, which was probably merely a passage between two parts of the palace. A fourth entrance could be gained through an 'emergency door' next to room 12.

I come next to the question of the island's suitability for habitation, bearing in mind its physical and geographical features. Geographically, the main features are:

1. Its situation at the extreme end of the water-way leading from the Far East, Southern Arabia and East Africa.

2. Its situation at the head of three land routes leading to Syria (through the Provincia Arabia), Palestine, Phœnicia and Egypt.

3. The arid nature of the island, and its comparative proximity to more fertile areas.

4. The fact, deriving possibly from the above, that with minor exceptions the island lay at the extreme geographical limit of political rule, whether of a small power or of a great empire (see Atlas of Israel, Sheet I/IX).

The island stood out by reason of its natural defensibility and safe harbour. It formed an ideal stronghold for the scattered, semi-nomadic population based on the few watering points along the shores of the Gulf of Eilat (Aqaba).

Consideration of the features we have mentioned suggests that the island's population would have varied both in extent and character through the ages. We can assume that at different times the island would have been used as a fishermen's and seamen's settlement, as an asylum for the nomadic herdsmen of the mainland, as a commercial centre linking the overseas countries with the continents to the north, as a port where sea-borne merchandise could be safely stored before being re-routed by caravan, as a base of operations against Red Sea pirates, as a post for a garrison or for custom officials, or even as a winter resort or place of confinement for notables.

The remains at ground level are to be associated with activities of a peaceful nature. The lower wall was designed to give protection for a community of some considerable size and would have required a large garrison to guard its length of 900 yards or more. The buildings on the hill-top were primarily of a military character.

The most suitable area for a residential quarter was at H (the only other flat piece of ground, by the harbour, was occupied by warehouses). We can envisage the first settlement of the island taking place at H, on hill B and around the harbour and port. An increase in commerce with southern countries (as in late Roman and Byzantine times) would lead to an increase in population. The quantities of valuable transit goods stored in the port and the growing danger from pirates would have necessitated the building of the wall.

The Islamic conquests changed the political constellation prevailing in this part of the world, and from an important link between two continents Jeziret Fara'un sank into an insignificant frontier post. The dwindling population would tend to concentrate on the hills.

We know that in the time of the Crusaders Renaud de Châtillon used the island as a base for piratical operations against the Red Sea coast of Arabia. The role of the island in the naval skirmishes with the Portuguese pirates who invaded the Red Sea in the 16th and 17th centuries is uncertain.

The better preserved buildings date from comparatively recent times and were probably used as a base of operations against smugglers or as a safe maritime station for Ottoman officials. The possibility that an independent sheikh used the island as a base is worth investigating (a parallel would be Dahr el Amer's use of the fort of Jidin in Galilee in the 18th century).

While assumptions based on architectural evidence could be used as starting points in an investigation of the island's history, only historical and archaeological research would enable us to say whether the island of Fara'un was occupied for a considerable length of time, whether the main area of settlement was at H and in the harbour area, and whether the island was an important station on the south–north trade routes.

LIST OF PLATES

LIST OF FIGURES

The scale measurements on the Figures are in Metres